The Malt Whisky Guide

THE MALT WHISKY GUIDE

Making
Whisky Fun

David Stirk

Author - David Stirk

Photography - Graeme & Derek Wallace

Design - Kevin Jeffery

Reprographics - LC Reprographics

Printing - Twenty 20 Ltd

Published by

GW Publishing

2 Telford Road
Houndmills, Basingstoke
Hants RG21 6YU

Tel 01144 1256 814060

First Published 2002

Copyright GW Publishing

Photography Copyright Graeme & Derek Wallace

Publishing

ISBN   Hardback 0 9535397 2 5 Leather 0 9535397 3 3
Paperback 0 9535397 4 1

To register for revisions of this book and future publications
or to order additional blank tasting pages please visit our website

www.gwpublishing.com

The Malt Whisky Guide is the combined effort of author David Stirk whose style and tastings are rapidly gaining popularity and recognition; along with Graeme & Derek Wallace whose photography has appeared in numerous publications including National Geographic.

The object of this book is to encourage more people to enjoy single malt whisky, and to encourage those who have already been won over to the cause to experiment with new expressions and record their findings. As David Stirk points out within the book, malt whisky is a fascinating yet peculiar drink. So much can be found within its complex make up, yet people may totally disagree with each other on what they find. Even the distillers cannot totally explain why one malt will vary with another since there are so many factors that contribute to the final product.

The book is informative in an informal way and supported by colourful and interesting photography of each distillery and the distillation process. The tasting notes have been restricted to malts which are fairly easy to find and are supported by images of the bottle and packaging. Finally at the back of the book there is a section for you to record your own notes. We encourage you to try your hand at recording your findings then comparing them with David's tasting notes.

Three formats are available, paperback or as a hardbound or leather personal organiser that allows for expandability and for you to add or reprioritise your tastings in alphabetical order along side the authors.

Please take some time to visit our web site and register your details so that we may advise you of future revisions or publications. You can also order additional loose-leaf blank tasting note pages from the site. Visit www.gwpublishing.com

We hope our book will result in your trying new malts and compiling your findings.

Have fun.

Anthracite at Balvenie

David is the previous Tastings Coordinator for Whisky Magazine and has had several articles including lifestyle, consumer and technical pieces printed in the magazine. He has sat on whisky tasting panels for Whisky Magazine and Which? Magazine in both cases trying to discover which whisky was the greatest in the world !

Currently David can be found at most of the whisky festivals throughout the world holding tastings and giving talks. He is also the Sales & Marketing Executive for Cadenhead's Independent Bottlers. David lives in Campbeltown and survives there despite possessing an outrageous English accent.

For my dad.

Who has to take some of the blame for my introduction into single malt whisky

David Stirk

PLEASE BEAR IN MIND THAT THE COMMENTS AND TASTING NOTES WITHIN THIS BOOK ARE MY OWN PERSONAL VIEW AND ARE NOT INTENDED TO DISCREDIT ANY PARTICULAR BRAND OR EXPRESSION. THE BEAUTY OF SINGLE MALT WHISKY IS THAT IT IS A COMPLEX SPIRIT AND WHAT ONE PERSON DETECTS MAY OFTEN BE COMPLETELY DIFFERENT TO ANOTHER. WE ALL HAVE DIFFERENT TASTES AND WILL DIFFER IN PREFERRED STYLES OF WHISKY, BUT IF THIS WEREN'T THE CASE THEN WE WOULD NOT HAVE THE TREMENDOUS SELECTION WE ARE ABLE TO ENJOY TODAY.

THE WHOLE PURPOSE OF THIS BOOK IS TO ENCOURAGE YOU TO GO OUT AND TRY THE DIFFERENT SINGLE MALTS FOR YOURSELF, DRAW YOUR OWN CONCLUSIONS AND ENJOY THE EXPERIENCE IN THE PROCESS.

Malt whisky is a young man's drink, contrary to popular wisdom. I discovered it at 19, and so did David Stirk.

When I set about visiting distilleries and making tasting notes on their whiskies, I was told that this was a pointless exercise. In a majority of cases, I was assured the distilleries would soon close permanently. In the meantime, their products were impossibly hard to find beyond the Highlands. Nobody had attempted quite such a task, so there was no book on the scale that I planned. "That is because there is no market for this kind of information," I was told by prospective publishers. Fortunately, I exhibited the tenacity with which every Yorkshireman is blessed.

David Stirk is also from Yorkshire. In 1999, in aid of the charity Mencap, he toured all 88 working distilleries in Scotland in five days. Now he has turned his tenacity to the writing and production of this book. Publishers no doubt told him there are now too many books on the subject. I hope he explained to them why his is different: its emphasis on malts that are readily available; its breezy, youthful writing style; a loose-leaf system that can be updated with your own notes and David's future tastings.

I am flattered David describes me as his literary mentor. I didn't know I played that role in David's life, but I shall encourage him to further tenacity. Many of those "impossibly hard to find" whiskies are now widely available. There is further tasting to be done. I'm up for it. So is David.

How about you?

Don't forget your Malt Whisky Guide.

Michael Jackson

*Michael Jackson is the world's best-selling and most widely published, writer on whisky, His Malt Whisky Companion (Dorling Kindersley) is now in its fourth edition.

I discovered the delights of single malt whisky in Shipley, Yorkshire near where I was born. At the tender age of 19 I shouldn't have had Glenlivet 21 year-old wasted on me but I am very grateful it was. The first bottle I bought was The Balvenie 10 year-old; the next was Laphroaig 10 year-old. Perhaps all introductions into malt whisky should take the same route!

Malt whisky is perhaps the most ambiguous and indescribable drink in the world. The only other drinks in the world that are indescribable are Coca-cola and Dr Pepper (if you don't believe me try and describe them). Since though, neither of these sugar-intense soft drinks offers any sort of complexity or ambiguity (there's that word again) it was decided that this book better be about single malt whisky.

There are certain distilleries not represented and none of the independent bottlers have been included. The reason for the omissions of certain distilleries is due to the fact that they either do not bottle a single malt whisky or have discontinued the expression they were bottling. Many more of the distilleries are also either mothballed, are in the process of being mothballed or are demolished. Some of the whiskies listed in the book will only be around a few more years, others a bit longer.

This isn't meant to sound overly negative; well a bit maybe, never the less, the industry has also seen some bold and buoyant moves over the last decade. Three new distilleries and countless purchases, restorations and new bottlings have stolen the industry's headlines. It is the time for the independent bottler to nibble away at the scraps left by one of the many huge companies that control the industry. Benromach, Bruichladdich, Bladnoch, Tomintoul and Speyside have all gained new owners and will begin to shine in the next decade (some even earlier).

This book is meant to guide you into the world of malt whisky and what is readily available and there is enough here to keep anyone going for a lifetime. Don't take my notes too seriously; rather make and enjoy your own notes, at your own pace. Then share them with a friend over a dram of one of your favourites. After all, there is no such thing as bad whisky, just some that you prefer more than others!

CHRONOLOGY:

1494 - First record of the production of aqua vitae by a Friar John Coll.

1505 - Barber Surgeons in Edinburgh granted a monopoly of distilling aqua vitae.

1644 - Charles I imparts a tax of 2s 8d on every Scots pint (about 1/3 of a gallon) of aqua vitae sold within the country.

1707 - The Treaty between England and Scotland brings Scottish tax in line with English tax and a new Malt Tax is introduced.

1725 - Malt taxed again in Scotland.

1736 - Earliest known reference to 'whisky'.

1781 - Private distilling banned.

1784 - The Wash Act defines the Highland Line.

1788 - Duties again increased on whisky.

1823 - A new act enables distillers to go legal for £10 a year.

1830 - Aeneas Coffey develops the Coffey Still.

1853 - The first blend, Ushers is introduced.

1870 - Phylloxera vastatrix destroys the vineyards of France.

1877 - The Distillers Company Ltd is formed.

1898 - Pattison crash.

1906 - Islington Council case "What is Whisky?" begins.

1908 - The Royal Commission decides both grain and malt distillations can be called whisky.

1909 - Whisky is defined as a "spirit obtained by the distillation of a mash of cereal grains saccharified by the diastase of the malt; that Scotch whisky is, as above defined, distilled in Scotland." Lloyd George, in favour of the Temperance Movement, raises taxes on whisky.

1920 - Prohibition starts in America.

1933 - The repeal of prohibition.

1947 - Taxes increased on whisky.

1960 - Formation of the Scotch Whisky Association.

1991 - EC regulations enshrine the concept that Scotch whisky is spirit elaborated from a grain alcohol, matured for at least three years in casks in Scotland and marketed at at least 40%.

Distilling 'uisge beatha' (the origin of the word whisky) was a way of life for the Scottish people. Crofters would often distil the leftover grain from a good harvest, and in later times found a market for distilled grains and a way to profit from the land. The whisky of this day was harsh and full of impurities, sold often straight from the still. The process of maturing had not been conceived and whisky was 'tampered' with in order to take away the extreme taste (in the same way gin was). Anything from spices, herbs, heather and even honey was added to make whisky taste good. The 'cratur' our ancestors drank was pretty mean stuff as recorded by Martin Martin at the end of the 17th Century:

"Several sorts of liquors, as common Usquebaugh, another called Trestarig... three times distilled, which is strong and hot; a third sort is four times distilled and this by the natives is called Usquebaugh-baul... which at first taste affects all the members of the body: two spoonfuls of this last liquor is a sufficient dose; and if any man exceed this, it would presently stop his breath, and endanger his life."

Long before the English government tried to control, or rather tax, the distilled products of these crofters, the Scottish government, due to some very poor harvests, had already tried banning the distillation of grain that could be used for food. Such was the mentality of the people at these times that the commands of the government to stop distilling to help save the starving often fell on deaf ears.

This was perhaps the beginning of the belief that whisky was evil and should be controlled; an image that whisky still has even today in some parts of the world. The truth of the matter was that there was no control over the manufacture or consumption of uisge beatha and consequently it was taken for granted. That was until after a spate of failed attempts to tax the distillers to the teeth (often to gain revenue to fight wars or recovery from a defeat) the government with the help of the Duke of Gordon, passed the Excise Act in 1823. This act was the beginning of the end of illicit distilling and was key to shaping the industry into what it is today; the second largest export from Scotland and Britain's fifth largest industry.

After the passing of the 1823 act several distilleries immediately obtained a license, although there were a number of licensed distilleries before this date. Glenlivet was one of the first distilleries to be licensed under the Excise Act and George Smith, Glenlivet's founder, consequently came under heavy fire (literally) from illegal distillers who resented his decision to start paying the English government for the right to perform a task that was every Scot's given right.

The Excise Act had an immediate effect and before the close of 1825, 152 new distilleries had been licensed. Landowners not only encouraged their crofters (who were distilling illegally anyway) to take out a license but were also building distilleries themselves in what was the first distillery boom. Some of these landowners had little or no experience in the manufacture and selling of the whisky and either employed illicit distillers to run their distilleries or simply failed.

It was around this time that a number of discoveries and techniques were discovered in the production of whisky. In the "Memoirs of a Highland Lady", Elizabeth Grant of Rothiemurchus gives the first indication that the concept of maturing whisky had been discovered. It would appear from her account that whisky was aged for a few years and was 'mild as milk' although she also relates to the whisky being 'long in uncorked bottles' which would suggest that most of the heavier alcohols will have evaporated (if you don't believe me leave out a glass of whisky overnight and try it in the morning). The practice of maturing whisky also seems to be only possible for affluent consumers as the vast majority of the whisky was being sold and drunk hot off the still.

Another breakthrough was the opening of the English, and to a lesser extent, the Irish markets for the exportation of Scotch. This was a new concept before the whisky boom of the 19th Century, not only did Scotland consume a very large percentage of its own whisky but it was importing great quantities of spirit from England. There was already a difference set up by this time between grain and malt spirit. Grain spirit had been for a long time distilled traditionally in the Lowlands by whisky dynasties such as the Steins and the Haigs in large copper stills. However, as the market possibilities grew in the south both malt and grain spirit was being sought after for rectification into gin (as gin was the gentleman's drink at the time).

The large copper pot stills were slow and cumbersome however needing constant recharging, cleaning and maintenance. Robert Stein invented the continuous still in 1827 although it was William Haig who first installed one in his Cameronbridge Distillery; Andrew Stein followed in 1828 installing his still in his Kirkliston Distillery.

All of this expansion and increase of capacity meant that for the first time the market was saturated with stocks of whisky. Although the markets in England and Ireland had risen, manufacturers were still unable to find a method for exporting the whisky overseas. Over the next few years several large dynasty's collapsed as their agents could no longer move their stock and the high overheads dragged the companies into bankruptcy. Both the Steins and the Haigs businesses went under although the Haigs were able to pay off their creditors - the name Haig would reappear in whisky in a big way.

Whilst the industry was going through its worst shake-up an ex-Inspector General of Excise in Dublin was perfecting the Stein Still. Aeneas Coffey, inventor of the Coffey still, perfected his still in 1830 although did not see it working until 1834. The still was capable of working off 3,000 gallons of wash an hour and meant an incredible amount of whisky could be made in a very short space of time. At first Coffey took his idea to the great whisky houses in Ireland but was met by traditionalism and cynicism. The Irish were going to stick to their pot still whisky and had no room for a mass-producing, flavour-reducing still. This was to be their downfall and Irish whisky suffered in a way that is too painful to go into detail.

The Scots took the Coffey still right to their hearts straight away and the first still went up in the Grange Distillery in Alloa, Clackmannanshire in 1834. Although this investment turned out to be disastrous with the owner of the Grange Distillery being sequestrated in the same year as the installation of the still. The first step had been made and soon others followed. By 1836 the Coffey stills was accounting for 29% of all grain whisky made in Scotland and things would never be the same again.

There is a myth surrounding malt whisky that claims the only reason why it suffered before the latter half of the 20th Century is that grain whisky was so much cheaper and faster to produce. That is only a half-truth as consumers were also warded off malt whisky due to its harshness. Even today the world trend for spirit drinkers is edging toward white spirits; neutral spirits that can be distilled in your bathroom and drunk straight away (preferably with something sweet and carbonated to give it flavour and texture). What was discovered with grain whisky was that the rectification process was not only easier to manage but also made a lighter and easier to swallow drink. This opened up the markets for the drinker of gin, brandy and other easy to swallow drinks.

This success was not overnight however. After the rush for distillery licenses as a result of the Excise Act in 1823 distilleries were finding times difficult. Over production was rife throughout the industry with little planning about how or when the surplus stocks would be sold. Even the Talisker Distillery, already famous for its quality, came up for sale at £1,000 in 1855. The new grain distillers with their mass-producing Coffey stills were one cause of the over production being able to distil in one month what most distilleries produced in a year.

Blends bridged the gap for the drinker outside of Scotland: Take a lot of grain spirit, add a little of the harsh Highland stuff (as most of the grain whisky was distilled south of the Highland line) and sell it as pure Scotch whisky; make no claim or allusion to a great taste only that the quality will speak for itself. The concept was simple and brilliant and hence took the world by storm. This one development, above all others, threw whisky into the limelight like no other drink the world has seen.

Andrew Usher is credited with bottling or marketing the first blend in 1853 and many others soon followed suit. Many of the blends that are household names today arose from blending companies created in the mid to late 19th Century. Names such as Dewar's, Haig, Famous Grouse and Bells were all followers of the belief that blends would conquer the English market, and later the world.

Assisting whisky to its meteoric rise in fame was the phylloxera aphis - a bug that attacks the roots and foliage of vines. First detected in 1863 in the Rhone Valley, the phylloxera aphis spread rapidly throughout the wine regions of France, Spain and Portugal destroying the vast vineyards. Towards the end of the 1879's the bug had devastated the claret trade and output of cognac fell by more than two-thirds from 1880 to 1900.

The English had been good customers to the cognac trade who were now dangerously low on stock. In order to satisfy their thirst the English turned to the new, trendy blends and vatted malts. This was the signal for unprecedented growth. Capitalising on the growth and ensuring steadier control over the future the Distillers Company Ltd (DCL) was formed in 1877. The company was an amalgamation of the large grain distillers; Cambus, Cameronbridge, Carsebridge, Glenochil, Kirkliston and Port Dundas.

The Distillers Company Ltd was initially set up to control the manufacture and supply of grain whisky although this strategy dramatically changed with the crash of Pattisons Ltd of Leith in 1898. The firm of Pattisons was similar in most respects to the other great blending houses of the time and had the company been a little shrewder in their business the crash may well have been avoided. It was however, the lavish lifestyle of the owners of Pattisons that first raised suspicion and then forced the company into bankruptcy. The company was already an aggressive advertiser before it tripled advertising to £60,000 in 1898. Everything about the company exuded confidence and success and this coupled with the state of the market and rising prices for whisky caused bank loan after bank loan to be approved.

When the firm finally crashed in December 1898 the repercussions were felt throughout Scotland. Attempts were made to reconstruct the business, as it was believed that the liquidation of the company's assets would release such high levels of stock into the market. These apprehensions were not realised, as assets were valued at less than half the value of the £500,000 debt Pattisons had ended with.

The Pattison crash did not devastate the whisky industry to the extent that experts had predicted. Despite many businesses throughout the industry collapsing, the major players rode the storm and concentrated on ensuring that the industry did not suffer at the hands of spurious investors in the future. The major outcome from the Pattison crash was the change in strategy by the DCL who began to purchase failing malt distilleries from the Highlands.

This wasn't before a small borough of London took up the challenge to define whisky for the first time. The entire case was brought about due to the decision of the Islington Borough Council to prosecute two wine merchants for the sale of whisky 'not of the nature, substance and quality demanded'. Although the case highlighted the mass adulteration of spirits throughout the United Kingdom the real case was fought over the percentage, if any, of grain whisky to malt whisky in a blend that should be vatted.

The blenders sided with the grain distillers insisting that whisky could be made from any grain and more importantly whisky would not be as widely drunk if the milder grain whisky was not added to the harsher malt from the Highland pot distilleries. In retaliation to the malt distillers the DCL, who were footing the costs of the legal battle in defence of grain whisky, bottled the first ever single grain whisky 'Cambus'. Cambus was seven years old and was advertised as having 'Not a Headache in a gallon." This slogan was due to medical belief at the time that it was the impurities in the malt whisky that caused hangovers and headaches.

The Borough of Islington at first sided with the malt distilleries decreeing that 'Irish or Scotch whisky meant a spirit obtained in the same methods by the aid of the form of still known as the pot still.' This judgement greatly alarmed the grain distillers who had installed and were using patent stills. Eventually a Royal Commission was set up to answer the question "What is whisky?" The answer came in 1909 when the Commission judged whisky to be "spirit obtained by the distillation of a mash of cereal grains saccharified by the diastase of the malt; that Scotch whisky is, as above defined, distilled in Scotland."

The outcome of the Royal Commission was slightly muted due to the budget announced by the Chancellor of the Exchequer Lloyd George. George was in favour of the temperance movement and used his position to try and fight the gross over consumption of alcohol that gripped the UK. The extra taxes coupled with a slowing economy hit the whisky industry hard. From 1909 to 1912 the number of working distilleries fell from 142 to 120, which affected all of the blending houses and subsidiaries.

Even with the outbreak of the First World War Lloyd George continued his personal campaign against distillers. He announced: "Drink is doing more damage in the war than all the German submarines put together" Protests to George's suggestions came from the Irish Nationalist members and the whisky trade. It had long been believed by the temperance movement that young spirit caused more drunkenness than spirit that had been aged for a period of time. In order to appease Lloyd George the whisky industry agreed for the first time to have a mandatory period of 3 years ageing before whisky could be called Scotch.

The war more than hampered the production of whisky with supplies being rationed and occasionally sunk by the German U-Boats. The Control Board, set up by Lloyd George to monitor and ration the activities of the distillers, did not help the industry imposing several restrictions throughout the war including periods when any form of distillation was banned. The board also encouraged the distillers to bottle their whisky at a lower alcoholic strength eventually allowing the distillers to bottle at a strength no greater than 40% alcohol.

Eventually in 1919 the ban on distilling was lifted and distilleries were allowed to trade overseas again. The government still did not see the benefit of the whisky industry and raised taxes once again. This led to more sales of blending houses and distilleries - once again the DCL mopped up the stricken companies. No sooner though had the war ended than a new opponent to the sales of Scotch threatened; prohibition. The temperance movement had only threatened to gain a majority on UK soil and had it not been for the aggressive measures set by Lloyd George, a pro temperance campaigner, would have caused little damage to the UK markets. In the new world power, USA, prohibition was finding favour in a people that had migrated on the back of religious differences.

Dallas Dhu Distillery, ceased production in 1983

Prohibition lasted for over 12 years although loopholes in the laws allowed whisky to be prescribed as a medicine, and smuggling allowed for a consistent amount of consumption of Scotch in the US. During these twelve years the whisky industry was hit harder by the deepening recession and the Wall Street crash than prohibition. Had the DCL not continued to buy-out blenders and distilleries and controlled the amount of production there is little doubt that the industry would not have survived World War 2.

From 1943 until August 1944 no whisky was made in the UK. This could well have been the case for the entire war had Winston Churchill not intervened; "On no account reduce the barley for whisky. This takes years to mature and is an invaluable export and dollar producer. Having regard to all our other difficulties about export it would be most improvident not to preserve this characteristic British element of ascendancy."

While this did not save the whisky industry a very difficult war period it certainly saved them from long periods of inactivity. After the war the home market had their supplies of whisky rationed as the government tried to maximise exports to gain revenue to repair it's broken cities. This was accepted through gritted teeth and production slowly rose and occasional re-openings were a glimmer of light in the otherwise grim news.

Slow growth quickly expanded and the first whisky boom for fifty years occurred with many distilleries being re-opened and others being built. The restrictions placed upon the whisky industry were relaxed and the US market began to soar. The home market was consuming more whisky and more whisky had to be made to fulfil orders coming from overseas.

The DCL had slowly become a major force in the whisky industry and to oppose their dominance new players emerged with the post war boom. Companies such as Seagram, Allied Domecq and the introduction of Japanese (and US) investors saw to it that many of the famous distillery names were owned by large conglomerates run overseas. Which brings the industry almost to the 21st Century. After the closures and downturn of production in the eighties, the industry recovered in the ninety's despite the recession and three new distilleries were built; Kininvie, Speyside and Arran.

The 21st Century has seen mergers and buy-outs that will affect the industry for decades to come. The emergence of Pernod Ricard as a major producer has come about sharply due to the sale of the spirits arm of Seagram's. The other two major companies Allied and United Distillers and Vintners (owners of DCL) have slowly been weeding out distilleries that cease to be needed. Mergers and buy-outs have forced UDV to sell certain distilleries to maintain a balance within the industry. A monopoly in their favour would not be healthy for the industry.

The most encouraging news from the Scotch industry has been the resurgence of smaller companies owning distilleries. All will be covered later in the book but it is these distilleries that tailor their whiskies to the consumers who will eventually succeed where others fail. The world market is showing a sharp increase in malt whisky drinkers and while the demand for blends decreases it will be the time for the pot distillers to have their revenge albeit over a century later.

The process of making whisky involves five stages; malting, mashing, fermentation, distillation and maturation and is made using only three ingredients water, barley and yeast. Each part of the process adds or removes certain flavours and allows the distiller a degree of control over how the finished product will taste. Despite great advances being made in the scientific understanding and implementation of the distilling process, very little has changed over the centuries.

MALTING

Barley - the only grain used in the production of single malt whisky.

Steeping - the process of raising the moisture content of the barley in order to allow germination to begin.

Germination - the growth of the grain into a plant. Germination breaks down the starch compounds so that they can be turned into sugar.

Kilning - the kilns dry the barley thereby arresting the germination process. Kilning is also responsible for most of the peaty flavour in whisky.

Malting floor at Laphroaig

Phenolic level - the degree of peatiness of the malt after being kilned.

Malt - barley that has begun the germination process but has not used the starch that will later be turned into sugar.

The malting of the barley was once the most labour intensive part of the distillery's work but is almost always now performed in large industrial maltings. Some distilleries such as Laphroaig, Bowmore, Springbank, Balvenie and Highland Park still carry out on-site, traditional floor-maltings but this is becoming more and more scarce.

Despite malting being carried out on an industrial scale it still follows the same principles as the traditional floor-maltings. The grain barley has to start the process of growing into a plant - or germination. For germination to begin three ingredients are required; air, water and heat.

The barley will arrive at the maltings plant with a moisture content of around 12%, which is too low for the germination of the grain to begin. The barley is 'steeped' in water until the moisture content is up around 40% at which time germination can often begin if the temperature is right. The temperature of the barley (now called a 'piece') must be controlled to avoid overheating, this is done by temperature humidified air being blown through the barley or by altering the depth when spread on a malting floor. The germination process takes anywhere from 7 to 12 days on a traditional malting floor or around 5 days in a mechanical maltings.

Germination is signalled by the growth of an 'acrospire' - a green rootlet growing from the base of the grain. The starch within the grain is what feeds the growth of the plant. The acrospire triggers the break down of the starch and therefore has to be halted once it has grown to about half the length of the grain, in order to maintain high levels of starch within the barley. If the acrospire grows too long then it will start to use it's own energy source thereby giving a smaller yield when it is 'mashed' which is the next process.

Halting the germination process is achieved by kilning - drying the malt. Kilns can be spotted at most distilleries by the distinct pagoda-shaped roofs that were introduced in the latter half of the 19th Century by the Elgin architect Charles Doig. The design was to aid the venting of the kilns, drawing the smoke through the malt and out of the top of the structure. The pagoda roofs became symbolic and distilleries have since been built utilising the design if only for aesthetic purposes. Inside these kilns peat and anthracite are fired under a fine mesh holding the malt. The amount of peat used in the kiln will determine the 'phenolic' level of the malt and distilleries can specify exactly the phenolic level for their malt.

The malt is then cleaned, removing part of the husk and the acrospire ready for milling. Milling is the most dangerous part of the distilling process as the fine powder from the malt is highly explosive and without care and attention small rocks that made it into the mill would spark and cause terrible explosions and fires. Much of the rebuilding of distilleries has been due to fires caused by mill explosions. The malt is not milled to the point of becoming flour; rather it is turned into 'grist' - a mixture of husk and flour.

Kiln floor

Loading the fire at Bowmore

MASHING

Grist - a mixture of coarse, medium and finely ground, malted barley

Mash tun - a large cylinder fitted with mechanical stirrers. Effectively a giant teapot.

Mashing - the process of extracting the sugar from malted barley using hot water.

Draff - what is left of the grist having had all of the sugar removed.

Wort - the brown, sweet liquid drained from the mash tun at the end of the mashing process.

Underback - the container that receives the wort ready for cooling.

MASH TUN

Tobermoray Mash Tun

The grist and hot water is poured into the 'mash tun' effectively a giant teapot. The mash tun has a perforated floor that allows the water to be drained while leaving the grist. Inside the mash tun there are also huge mechanical stirrers that mixes the water and the grist. The stirring and mixing with hot water extracts the sugar from the malt turning the liquid brown and leaving it quite sweet, surprisingly a little bit like barley water.

Inside Glen Garioch Mash Tun

Inside Bowmore Mash Tun

After about three hours the first water is drained, leaving the grist, and a second, even hotter water is added. The process of mashing is repeated and the water is then drained. The final stage is the adding of water that is almost boiling to the nearly spent grist. This water takes whatever sugars are left in the grist and is used as the first water for the next load. The spent grist is called 'draff' and is extracted from the mash tun often right into the back of a farmers truck to be used as cattle feed.

Using three stages for mashing enables distillers to extract as much of the sugar as possible from the grist. The brown, sweet liquid that is drained is called 'wort' and is deposited into an 'underback' before being cooled ready for the next stage; fermentation.

FERMENTATION

Washback - Large wooden or steel cylinders fitted with large beaters that act to beat down the froth of the fermenting wort.

Wash - Once the wort has begun fermentation and has an alcohol content, it is referred to as the wash.

The wort is cooled before filling a 'washback' to prevent killing the yeast that is added to enable fermentation. Most distillers use either a single distillers yeast or a mixture containing brewer's yeast. Once the yeast has been added there is a short quiet period (calm before the storm if you will) followed by a furious phase that rocks the lids of the washbacks. Many distilleries have beaters fitted that help keep the 'wash' from frothing over the top - a common problem.

Washbacks at Ardbeg

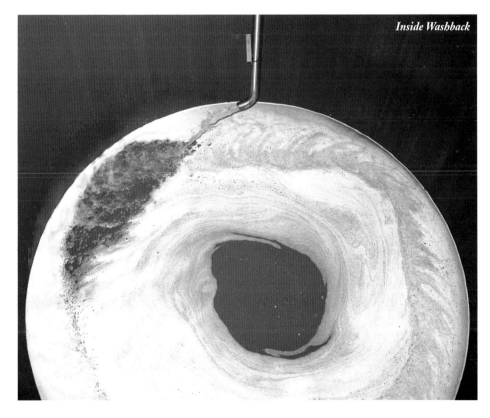

Inside Washback

The reaction of turning the sugar into alcohol creates enormous amounts of carbon dioxide and can become quite a health hazard. Whenever visiting a distillery be careful when breathing in the malty, yeasty aromas of the wash - your head will get quite a kick if you get too close. The whole fermentation process takes around 48 hours and leaves a weak beer with around 8% ethyl alcohol content.

Washback at Ardbeg

DISTILLATION

Stills at Jura

Wash still - distills the wash to about 22% alcohol.

Lyne arm - the sloping copper pipe fitted at the top of the still which leads to a worm tub or condensors.

Worm tub - a coiled copper pipe immersed in water within a large tub usually outdoors. The vapours from the still pass through the pipe, cool and condense back to a liquid.

Condensor - A copper cylinder housing dozens of straight copper pipes through which cold water flows. The vapours from the still pass through the cylinder, cool and condense back to a liquid.

Rummager - a rotating arm with chains, lining the inside of the still. The chain turns around and acts like a scraper.

Pot ale - the yeast rich residue of the wash after the first distillation. Pot ale is often added to the draff for farmers to feed to cattle.

Low wines - the spirit before it is distilled a second time.

Spirit still - the second still that distills the low wines. Spirit leaving this still is around 70% alcohol.

Spirit safe - a large box usually made of brass and glass that allows the distiller to view the spirit coming off the stills. Within the box is instrumentation that allows the distiller to measure alcohol content and temperature. The box was designed to prevent any workers having direct access to the spirit.

Inside Still

Foreshots - the heavier alcohols that are the first to be condensed and enter the spirit safe. This alcohol content is around 80% and carries undesirable flavour compounds and harmful chemicals.

Middle cut - the heart of the distillate which will later become whisky. Containing a desired portion of foreshots and feints. The alcohol content is around 70%.

Feints - the end portion of the distillate and along with the foreshots is collected and sent back to the wash still to be added with the next distillation.

A distillery's stills are by far the most photographed part of the whisky making process. Surprisingly though it is impossible to see just what goes on inside the great copper kettles. Copper was originally used because of its ability to be bent into shape and has become a tradition with all pot stills now being made of copper. It also acts as a catalyst, improving the clarity of the spirit. Copper does wear easily however and it is quite common to see stills laid waste or with great patches of repair work.

The wash is pumped into the 'wash still' and heated by either direct coal fires, gas or by steam. Inside the still the wash begins to boil and as alcohol has a lower boiling point than water the alcohol makes it over the top of the still into the 'lyne arm' and down through a 'worm tub' or condenser where the vapours become a liquid again but with a much higher alcohol content than the wash. The wash still is often fitted with a 'rummager' device that prevents the wash sticking to the side of the still. The remaining residue called 'pot ale' is often mixed with the draff and ends up back on the farm to be used as cattle feed.

Still heating system at Balvenie

The wash still works until almost all of the alcohol has been distilled and the new liquid is around 22% alcohol. Having passed through a 'spirit safe' the 'low wines' are then pumped into the 'spirit still' for the second distillation. Most whisky in Scotland is distilled twice. Some Lowland distilleries use triple distillation while at Springbank some of their

expressions are distilled two and half times. The second distillation is much like the first except that the alcohol content of the distilled liquor is now between 60-70% alchohol. As the alcohol evaporates it is condensed and sent through the spirit safe where the stillman watches and measures the alcohol content ready to redirect the 'middle cut' to the 'spirit receiver'.

Outdoor worm tubs at Glen Elgin

As the heaviest alcohols evaporate first and they carry undesired and harmful chemical compounds the distiller will wait until the alcohol of the spirit drops to around 75% before diverting the spirit to the spirit receiver. Each distillery has a different cut-off point and this will determine how heavy the whisky is before entering the cask. If a distillery were to take too small a middle cut then they would also create a rather flavourless spirit not unlike vodka. It is essential that a small amount of the 'foreshots' and 'feints' make it into the spirit receiver.

Once the distiller has his middle cut the rejected spirit is added to the next wash entering the wash still. Thus distilling is similar to mashing whereby it recycles the leftovers of the batch that was processed previously. From the spirit receiver the spirit is emptied into the spirit-filling vat, which can contain many different distillations. After a few days the spirit is filled into casks and is then ready for the longest part of the whisky making process; maturation.

Stillman John Edgar at Lagavulin

Spirit Safe at Glen Moray

MATURATION

Whisky can be filled into a variety of different cask sizes although all casks are made out of oak. The most common sizes of casks are hogsheads (around 50 gallons) and butts (around 100 gallons). Before the casks make it to the distillery they are often rebuilt and checked for holes and leaks. The casks are also organised into groups of first-fill, re-fill and second and third-fill. The casks arrive in Scotland having been used once before by either a winery or an American distillery. Since casks wear out and slowly lose their ability to colour and affect the whisky most don't get used more than two times by a Scotch distillery. The casks are often charred (burnt) on the inside, this releases carbon which helps mellow the whisky.

Cask filling at Glen Moray

Spirit Maturing at Bruichladdich

The casks must be racked in warehousing in Scotland where they sit undisturbed for at least three years. Many distilleries have modern climate controlled warehousing which can stack up to fifteen casks high, but most still have traditional 'dunage" warehouses where casks are stored up to three high. Constructed with thick stone walls and earth floors the temperature naturally remains cool, not fluctuating more than 6˚C. The traditional method of 'stowing' casks involves the construction of shelves on top of the bottom row of casks.

As the spirit matures the oak breathes and the liquid inside evaporates. Each year it is estimated that a single cask will lose around 2% of its volume in evaporation, reducing the alcoholic content by approximately 0.4% abv. The lost spirit is appropriately named the 'Angel's Share' (which feeds the un-angelic black fungus seen on warehouse walls and surrounding buildings) and is accounted for in a tax relief.

Fungus covered walls at Longmorn Distillery

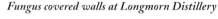

While we still know very little about what exactly occurs throughout the process of making whisky we do know that there are certain variables within the distiller's control to influence the overall taste of the whisky.

WATER

Water is by far the most important aspect to the success of a distillery. Without a clean and consistent supply of water any distillery is doomed. This may come as a strange warning to Scotland - a land that is no stranger to a bit of rain, but numerous distilleries have been shut down due to either lack of water or problems with water supply (sometimes even contaminated water).

There has been much discussion recently as to the addition of peat flavours in whisky due to the water used in the whisky making process. It is difficult to argue against some peat flavours finding their way into the finished product even when no peat is used in the kilning of the malt. Whiskies such as Tobermory, Glengoyne and Bunnahabhain all consistently have a slightly smoky flavour despite being made with malt that has a very low (almost zero) phenolic level.

So if water can be linked to peaty flavours in whisky then the other possibilities are almost endless. Perhaps grassy, earthy and some floral flavours could be the result of the type of water used? Recent research by Peter Hinde of Bradford University into Humic Acids (which are often responsible for

colouring water and imparting peaty flavours) has shown that water is susceptible to infinite climate changes that directly alter the flavour of water. This means that each collection of water used by a distillery is different in flavour from the next; for example, heavy rain can often mean peatier water.

PEAT

Many parts of Scotland are covered with peat bogs or moss. Peat is Vegetable matter that has decomposed in water and partly carbonised, many centuries are required for this natural process to take place. Peat is basically earth that can be cut, dried and used as fuel. Different areas of Scotland produce varying types of peat due to the variations in climate and flora and fauna.

Peat is the most obvious variable in the flavouring of whisky. Before the introduction of technologically advanced industrial maltings the peatiness of whisky was achieved through human judgement and controlled to a certain degree by the elements. Up until the discovery of coal all whisky was heavily peated as this was the only fuel used to fire kilns. With the introduction of coal distillers were given an option in the firing of their kilns and thus the peatiness of the whisky.

Since it was discovered that the mass market for whisky preferred the less fiery tasting whiskies, using heavily peated malt went out of fashion. The large blenders that dominated the whisky market only required a very small amount of peaty whisky to flavour their blends. Nowadays peaty whisky is in vogue and distillers are not only resurrecting past distilleries that made a peaty whisky they are also using their existing distilleries to create a peaty whisky to keep up with demand.

BARLEY

There are scores of different types of barley and every now and again farmers will switch the type of barley they grow to accommodate the distillers who desire barley suitable for distilling. Some of the flavours that are given from the barley are very obvious (e.g. malt and wheat flavours) others are not. Not much notice is given to the type of barley used and only Glengoyne and Macallan make a point of using one type of barley religiously. Their use of Golden Promise is dwindling however as most farmers have moved onto a different strain of barley that the other distilleries are requesting.

SIZE/SHAPE OF STILL

Very little is known about how altering the size of still affects the taste of whisky. There are certain reactions that take place between the copper and the spirit and it is believed that those distilleries that still use copper worm tubs get something that other distilleries do not. What the extra something is no one can pinpoint - whisky is not an exact science!

The shape of the still varies from small light bulb shapes to long elegant swan necks (and everything in between). Some argue that having smaller stills (such as Glenfiddich and Macallan), allows greater contact between the spirit and the copper while others claim that large stills (such as Glenfarclas and Jura) cause the spirit to be purer. Nothing is certain as both Macallan and Glenfarclas make a heavy spirit (regardless of the use of sherry casks - see Wood) and Jura and Glenfiddich make similar whiskies with regard to body.

What is generally believed is that the taller the still the lighter the alcohols have to be to pass onto the lyne arm. Although the slope of the lyne arm can often be more of a clue to how heavy the spirit is likely to be; the sharper the slope the more likely that more alcohol will make it to the cask.

The acute lyne arms at Lagavulin

WOOD

Maturation is perhaps the most mysterious part of the whisky making process. Whisky leaves the spirit still as a clear liquid with certain flavours and characteristics and several years later emerges from the insides of a cask a metamorphosed drink. Not too much is known about the chemical reactions that occur between the whisky and the oak that houses it and reports will often surface that contradict one another.

There are two types of oak that are commonly used and they are generically referred to as American and European oak. For the purpose of the tasting notes I have referred to the casks as ex-sherry (European oak) and ex-bourbon (American oak). American oak grows tall and straight, which is ideal for making casks. American producers of whisky are only allowed to mature their spirit in brand new casks by law. This means that each year there are thousands of new casks available for the Scotch whisky producers who prefer used casks. The casks are broken down into staves and then reassembled in cooperages in Scotland.

European oak goes through a similar process but very rarely ages spirit and instead houses either fermenting or ageing wines. These casks usually spend two years in a winery before being shipped across to Scotland either in similar packs as the ex-bourbon casks or as whole casks. Ex-sherry casks are usually the shape of butts and are around 3 - 4 times more expensive than ex-bourbon casks. Their availability is becoming more and more scarce as new methods of ageing wine become fashionable and also because sherry is becoming less popular.

Scotch whisky is almost always aged in used casks as it is deemed that the light spirit made in Scotland is not suitable for the heavy flavours that come from the new wood. Recently however distilleries like Glenfiddich and Glenlivet have finished their whiskies in brand new casks with mixed results. My prediction is that in the next decade this trend will take off as brand new casks become cost effective.

Malcolm Macdonald repairing cask at Glen Moray

The effect that the cask has on the whisky is also unknown. Some reports claim that the previous inhabitant of the cask will not influence the flavour of the whisky. I claim that this is nonsense and that colour, taste and smell are all influenced by the previous contents of the cask. Any number of the recent wood finishes backs up this claim and if it mattered little about the previous contents why are some distilleries so specific about how and who uses their casks before them?

All of the whisky tasted within this book has been expertly vatted from several hundred casks of the same malt whisky. A trip to any shop that stocks independent bottlings demonstrates how different each and every cask of malt whisky is. Some are incredibly colourless while others are almost black. It cannot be assumed either that just because the whisky in the bottle is dark is due to it being matured in ex-sherry casks. If that is the case why is bourbon whiskey so dark?

Scotch whisky has to be matured for at least three years although very little single malt whisky is bottled at this age. Most single malt whisky is aged for ten years as it is deemed a good age for most whisky to be bottled at. There is much debate regarding the relevance of location for the maturing of casks. Some feel that due to the fact that casks breathe, the whisky inside can take on some flavour characteristics of the air that surrounds it. Most distilleries near or next to the sea are very keen to mature their whisky next to the sea in the hope that this will allow certain aromas and tastes to make their way into the whisky.

Glenfiddich Warehouse

SCOTCH WHISKY

Whisky that can call itself 'Scotch' must be distilled and matured for no less than three years in Scotland. The title does not guarantee quality due to the enormous amount of Scotch available all over the world bottled by hundreds of different companies.

SINGLE MALT WHISKY

Also referred to as 'self', 'single', 'malt', 'pure malt' and 'pot-still'. Single malt whiskies are made entirely from malted barley and are the product of one distillery only.

GRAIN WHISKY

Grain whisky is made from a mixture of malted barley and other grains the most common of which is corn (maize). The malted barley is needed to create the enzymes that break down the starch compounds in the grain. The split is usually around 30% malted barley and 70% other grains.

BLENDED WHISKY

A blended whisky is made from a mixture of malt whisky and grain whisky. A blend can contain any percentage of either grain or malt whisky although it is generally perceived that the more expensive the blend the greater the percentage of malt whisky.

VATTED WHISKY

A vatted whisky can be either a vatted grain whisky or a vatted malt whisky. The vatting of different distilleries grain whiskies together or malt whiskies together (but not mixing grain whisky with malt whisky) is fairly rare but new companies such as Compass Box have begun a trend that is taking favour with consumers. Some companies have vatted enormous numbers of different whiskies together to celebrate dates and occasions. Chivas Regal bottled the Century of Malts that had 100 different single malt whiskies vatted and Gordon & MacPhail bottled the MacPhail 2000 - a vatted bottling with the combined ages of the whiskies vatted equalling 2000 years.

CASK STRENGTHS

Companies such as Cadenhead's and Glenfarclas prompted the trend of bottling whisky at cask strength; at 60% vol Glenfarclas' 105 was for a while the strongest whisky on the market. The rise of the independent bottlers has seen a similar rise in cask strength whiskies. The extra alcohol can make the whisky hard to swallow (or even get near to the nose) but it does allow the whisky to be judged before any adulteration takes place.

SINGLE CASKS

Bottling from a single cask has been pioneered by the independent bottlers but has been followed closely by the producers also. The problem for producers in bottling single casks is that there is no chance for consistency in the whisky. Each and every cask that matures will offer a different tasting whisky. Producers will often vat hundreds of casks to maintain consistency in their single malt whiskies. In bottling single casks the consumer is exposed to the huge differences that each cask may hold. Thus reputations can be made or ruined from the tasting of individual casks.

VINTAGES

Vintage whiskies are those that carry the year of distillation on their label, for example Glen Rothes 1987. Unlike wine where the word vintage can be used to do describe a 'good year', the quality of whisky is not subject to climate changes. If one year of a whisky happens to be better than another this will be due to any number of variables most notably being the vatting and the wood used for ageing, but unike wine not the climate.

WOOD FINISHES

This is the most recent development in the whisky industry allowing distillers a much greater degree of producing whiskies of a differing taste. It is unknown who started the trend of using different cask types (i.e. casks that had previously been used for ageing other alcoholic drinks) to impart flavours but Glenmorangie is credited with being the market leader in this field. The concept of flavouring whisky has left consumers divided. It is worth bearing in mind however that originally whisky was aged in any type of cask and ones that had been loaded with any type of cargo including salt, herrings and vinegar.

Independent bottlers purchase casks of whisky from brokers, private investors and distilleries. By bottling familiar and unfamiliar whiskies at odd ages and alcoholic strengths the independents are able to offer consumers a look at certain whiskies that the distilleries would not be able to do themselves. Over the past ten years the number of independent bottlers has escalated as more companies try to take advantage of the growing market interest in speciality whiskies. Most of the new companies have concentrated on single malt whiskies although there has been a large increase in the number if grain whiskies and vatted whiskies that have appeared from the independents.

ADELPHI DISTILLERY COMPANY

A recently rejuvenated whisky company, the Adelphi Distillery Ltd has been restored by the great-grandson of the original owner of the Adelphi Distillery. In its current guise Adelphi has taken advantage of the new consumer trend towards single cask strength unadulterated whiskies and this it is doing with distinction. Adelphi under the name Limerick, were the first to bottle Irish grain whiskey and as an independent the first to bottle Irish single malt.

BLACKADDER INTERNATIONAL

Blackadder is a small mail order and Travel Retail whisky company that was started by Robin Tucek and John Lamond although is now solely run by Robin Tucek. Despite the founder being based in Sweden all of the bottling is overseen and great care is given not to over filter the whisky. Blackadder insists that whisky should be bottled as naturally as possible despite this leading to some consumers wondering why there are bits of oak floating in the bottle. The result is a drinking experience that is difficult to match. Much of the Blackadder whisky goes overseas and is quite sought after in countries such as the USA and Japan.

COMPASS BOX DELICIOUS WHISKY COMPANY LTD

One of the newest independent bottlers although by far the loudest and boldest. Founded by John Glaser, previously with UDV, on a premise that people will drink anything if it tastes good and ekes quality and style. Compass Box is a small company with just a few bottlings available but given time the whisky with names such as 'Hedonism' and 'Eleuphera' will be in every bar and shop that matters.

CADENHEAD

Despite being owned by J & A Mitchell who also own Springbank Distillery, Cadenhead is run as a separate company. Cadenhead has four shops of its own in Campbeltown, Edinburgh, Covent Garden and Germany. As the oldest independent bottler in the world Cadenhead has around 140 different whiskies available at any given time. Cadenhead also specialise in bourbon, gin and grain whisky. The shops are always worth a visit although be prepared to be tempted.

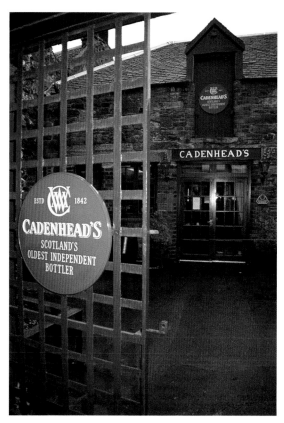

GORDON & MACPHAIL

The largest independent bottler in Scotland is responsible for continuing the availability of single malt whisky throughout numerous dark periods in whisky's history. Gordon & MacPhail are based in Elgin and until recently had never any part to play in the production of whisky being solely a buyer of casks and bottler of hard-to-find whiskies. That was until the company diversified and bought Benromach a local distillery that had been mothballed and dismantled by previous owners UDV. Gordon & MacPhail have vast stocks of distilleries produce, both present and past and shall continue to be a major force in the world of single malt whisky for many a decade to come.

SIGNATORY

The second largest independent bottler of whisky in the world, Signatory is owned and run by Andrew Symington, a man of seemingly endless energy and passion for the whisky industry. Trying to keep up with the stream of bottlings from Signatory is like trying to run next to a train. Signatory have the habit of every now and again bottling an extremely rare whisky such as Ben Wyvis and pricing it well within the collector's price range. The distinct gold 'S' that adorns Signatory's bottles is an assurance of value.

Every single malt whisky from Scotland is produced in one of five regions. The Highlands, Lowlands, Speyside, Campbeltown and the Islands. Somehow, over the course of the last century, or longer, we have been led to believe that these regions are responsible for producing markedly different flavoured whiskies. Or at least that the whiskies made within each region are similar in taste.

The truth of the matter is that there is no real correlation between the location and the taste characteristics of the whisky. The variables that exist within the control of the distiller and the ingredients required to make whisky are the reasons for the whisky tasting the way it does. However, the regions that exist do have other purposes other than categorising the taste characteristics of the whisky. For one, they are a handy way of roughly remembering whereabouts each distillery is located.

THE HIGHLANDS

This is the all-encompassing title given to all of the distilleries north of the Highland/Lowland line (split by the old borderline between Greenock on the Firth of Clyde in the west and Dundee on the Firth of Tay in the east), except those in Speyside. Thus the vast majority of mainland Scotland is described as the Highlands and includes the distilleries as far south as Loch Lomond, as far west as Oban, as far north as Old Pulteney and as far east as Fettercairn.

The cause of the Highland line coming to prominence was the split between initially the taxes paid above and below the Highland line and later the method of distilling as most grain distilleries were situated in or near the two biggest cities of Scotland; Edinburgh and Glasgow.

With the Highlands being so vast it is difficult to surmise the geography and style of a distillery you are likely to encounter. The journey to the Highland distilleries takes you in two directions; northwest towards Oban and Fort William, or northeast through the centrally located distilleries and then onto Montrose. Either direction leads you eventually towards the Muir of Ord and Inverness. From there you pass the Black Isle heading towards the Dornoch Firth and then finally finishing in Wick. On this journey it is possible to see just about everything the Scottish landscape has to offer.

THE LOWLANDS

Once the heart of the grain whisky industry, today the Lowlands is littered with streets named after distilleries and buildings, derelict and forlorn showing nothing of their former glory. Today only three Lowland distilleries are still active, Auchentoshan in Dumbarton, Glenkinchie in Pencaitland and Bladnoch, the most southerly Scotch distillery in Wigtown.

Perhaps the death of the Lowland industry has been the constant labelling by the media of their whiskies as light and girly (no offence meant). In fact much of their lightness has to do with the fact that they are traditionally triple distilled - in the same way that Irish whisky is supposed to be lighter. If you have ever had the chance to try Glenkinchie however, you will find a Lowland whisky can be just as heavy as the whiskies made up the road. It is nonsense that any minor climate change and/or the change in rock will have much say in how heavy the whisky will be.

ISLAY AND THE ISLANDS

Often referred to as simply Islay, which terribly undermines some of the greatest whiskies in the world. Indeed where would Highland Park be without the region of Islands? Surely not thrown into the vast Highlands?! It is often believed that the Islands give a seaside flavour to their whiskies, which only holds half an ounce of truth. If this was the case then distilleries such as Isle of Jura and Tobermory who show little hint of their location in their whiskies are using much greater filters on their whiskies than other distilleries.

The Isle of Islay is the focal point of the Islands region and has always been renowned as a centre for excellent whisky. Islay is just thirty-one miles across and has around 3,300 residents (the local phone book only lists a few hundred names). Yet the small island that was once part of the same landmass as Bushmills in Northern Ireland, is host to eight working distilleries and two others still standing.

Islay has seen the most immediate economic effects from the boom in single malt drinking. Up until 1996 there were only five working distilleries on Islay; Caol Ila, Bunnahabhain, Bowmore, Laphroaig and Lagavulin. In 1997 Glenmorangie plc bought Ardbeg Distillery from Allied Distillers and in 2001 a consortium led by Murray McDavid, the independent bottlers, bought Bruichladdich Distillery from JBB.

Islay is a fascinating island to visit and for many whisky enthusiasts it is a Mecca, and their journey a pilgrimage. It is sometimes hard to forget how difficult life on the island can be when confronted with the generosity and hospitality of the Ileach's - the people of Islay.

SPEYSIDE

Perhaps the most obvious choice for a region is that of Speyside. The area between Inverness and Aberdeen (roughly speaking although Royal Brackla and Glen Garioch are often labelled as Speyside when they are not) is home to more than 50% of all the Scotch whisky distilleries. None of these whiskies are heavily peated and most have a basic sweet, honeyish flavour (with perhaps a few notable exceptions). But at the same time this concentration of distilleries does more to ruin any thoughts of regionality than any other factor.

Speyside is home to a number of distilleries that sit side by side and yet make markedly different whiskies in some cases using the same slightly peated barley and the same water. How can you have regionality when this occurs? Many of the distilleries within Speyside also concentrate on producing one type of whisky. There is a group that concentrates on producing a light, floral whisky (take Cardhu, Benriach, Linkwood etc) and there are those heavyweights that insist on producing monstrously sweet, chewy whiskies (Macallan, Glenfarclas etc).

Neither whisky is more important than the other although most of us know which one sells better. Anyone who has drank Glenfiddich and Macallan hast to see the idiocy of insisting that categorising whisky by regions is a silly idea. However it is nice to be able to visit so many distilleries in such close proximity and Speyside is certainly unique in this regard.

CAMPBELTOWN

Once as thriving a whisky community as Speyside, Campbeltown suffered greatly due to crashes in the industry and poor grade whisky being associated with the region. This wasn't always the case and the Campbeltown revival, albeit in a small controlled way by J & A Mitchell is due to the quality of the whisky that the distilleries were capable of producing. Now, because of Springbank's refusal to compromise in areas of production where automation has taken over, Springbank whisky is in high demand and is continually voted by consumers as the best whisky available.

Unfortunately it is difficult to swallow the reasoning behind having a region that only has two working distilleries and four malts (Springbank makes three different malts; Springbank, Longrow and Hazelburn). Admittedly Glengyle has been revived but we will not see any results from this venture for at least ten years. But if there isn't a Campbeltown region does it get thrown into the Highlands, Lowlands or even Islands?

The tasting notes given in this book are not meant to confuse so I have tried to use a small group of words rather than describe a plethora of flavours. There are a few occasions where I have detected specific smells and flavours and have not been able to simplify the text. Much of this is irrelevant but it is important to understand where a few of my taste descriptors come from.

In order to better understand the flavours within a whisky it is helpful that the imbiber has visited a distillery in full production. Aromas from the malting, mashing, fermentation and distilling process can really only be found at a distillery. A tour of a distillery that allows you to taste the grain in different stages of malting, and nose some new-make spirit (spirit that has not been matured) is a must in order to identify some of the flavours that will arise in your glass of Scotch.

There are certain other words that often appear when whisky is being described. Some of these descriptors are born out of necessity; such as sherried (usually a word associated with a whisky that is predominantly aged in ex-sherry casks), bitter, sweet, sour and salty. The latter four are the four tastes of the mouth.

Other words crop up time and again when describing whisky due to their suitability. Such words are; christmas pudding or fruitcake, icing sugar, stewed fruits, licorice, caramel, heather, honey, citrus etc. These words are often used to describe a multitude of flavours that are easily summed up. The purpose of describing whisky after all is to help express what it tastes like to someone else, not confuse people by breaking down as many flavours as possible.

The greatest area of confusion when describing whisky lies in the detecting and deciphering of smoky smells. Phenols, or the smoky flavours, can be detected in an enormous variety of different aromas and tastes. Most of the phenolic aromas fall under three categories; peat, smoke, and tar and can be a combination of any number of the three.

What all of this flavour recognition and experience can lead to is an insatiable need to sniff everything around you. Whether it be the new brand of ketchup or the cat food, aroma is remembered in a way that is unknown to scientists and can be recalled decades after inhalation. Whisky will often remind you of something that has nothing to do with food such as leather or rubber but these aromas are not always undesirable, for example most of us love the smell of a new car; and so it can be with whisky.

Most of the consumption of whisky is carried out in your home, a bar or someone else's home (if you are fortunate with your choice of friends!). Therefore demanding that the guy with the beard in the corner of the bar stops smoking his pipe because he is messing about with your 'olfactory epithelium' will not wash. Drinking whisky is all about the pleasure you get from the drink. Noses can often be overrated (although I am at the front of the queue to tell anyone who will listen about the exceptional noses) - it is the hedonistic side of the drink that is THE most important aspect about malt whisky. Don't let anyone tell you otherwise - you know (or will hopefully find out) what you like and vice-versa, you know what you don't like.

Use my notes only as a guide. If I smell carrots and coriander and you don't, well who is to say who is right? My judgment will always be personal and I may sometimes remark on smells or tastes that you are not aware of (and vice versa). This book has a section for you to write your own notes for each whisky you try. I encourage you to try the same malt at different times of day or before and after a meal and you will be amazed at how you will detect different attributes even from the same malt. It may be fun to return to my tasting notes and see if we agree or not. I doubt we will agree all of the time and if we never agree any of the time - who cares? As long as you find a whisky you like, drink it and share it.

How to use this book and how to drink malt whisky (or any whisky) is quite simply answered however you see fit. It is now becoming an old cliche but the only way you should drink whisky is how you enjoy drinking whisky. I could tell you the benefits about watering down your whisky to open the bouquet (but I won't because I am not an advocate of that practice). And if I did tell you to add water, then how much do you add? You will have to find out for yourself through trial and error.

Everything about the way I nose and taste has come to me either by instinct or trial and error. The glass I use will depend upon the whisky I am drinking. Most of the time I use a wine nosing glass (because it is quite big and will hold lots of the cratur) or a Glencairn Blender's Nosing Glass. I like these glasses as they sit comfortably in the hand, are a nice weight and allow me to nose the whisky in the same way a wine nosing glass will.

Ian Morrison nosing at Macallan

Appreciating whisky will always, and must always be a personal thing. The key is not to take apart the process too much - trust me you will take the fun out of nosing and drinking whisky. Some will go to great lengths to describe the room, temperature, lighting, air-conditioning and so on in order to taste whisky. Unless you work for a large blending firm and are about to set the recipe for the next big blend I don't think much of the above is very important.

The whiskies are listed alphabetically for ease of reference and are not scored. My tasting notes are provided however to hopefully give you some idea of what to expect before buying your next whisky. I have shown my favourites as this will be of interest to some readers but of more interest I hope will be the chart categorising all of the whiskies tasted. This I hope will spark intrigue and discussion - for that is the real beauty of drinking whisky.

Light,
young, grassy,
perfumed

Light - medium,
sour fruits,
cereals

Light-medium,
malty, wine notes,
honey

Medium,
sherried, fruity,
malty, round

Medium,
peaty, fruity,
minty, briny

Medium - heavy,
rich, fruitcake, oak,
sherried, smoky

Medium - heavy,
strong peat, tar,
smoke

Arran*
Auchentoshan 10
Auchentoshan Select
Benriach 10
Cardhu 12
Dalwhinnie 15
Glen Grant
Glen Grant 10
Glen Moray
Glen Moray 12
Glen Moray 16
Oban 14
Rosebank 12
Tamnavulin 12

Aberlour 15
Ben Nevis 10*
Cnoc 12
Deanston 17
Glenfarclas 15
Glen Keith 10
Glenlivet 12
Glenrothes 1989
Glenturret 12
Glenturret 18
Inchmurrin
Knockando 1987
Linkwood 12*
Littlemill 8
Loch Lomond
Old Fettercairn 10
Old Rhosdhu 5

Aberfeldy 12
Auchentoshan 21
Balvenie 10
Benromach 18
Cragganmore 12
Dalwhinnie 1980 DE
Deanston 12*
Drumguish
Glenfiddich 12
Glenfiddich 18
Glengoyne 10
Glenlivet 12 American
Glenlivet 12 French
Glenmorangie 10
Glenmorangie 12
Glenmorangie 18
Glenmorangie Cellar13
Glenmorangie Madeira
Glenmorangie Trad
Glen Ord 12
Glenturret 15
Jura 10
Jura 16
Royal Lochnagar 12
Speyburn 10
Speyside 10
Strathisla 12
Tamdhu
Tomintoul

*My
Favourites

Aberlour 10*
Aberlour 1990
Aberlour a' bunadh
Auchentoshan Three*
Balblair 16*
Balblair Elements
Balvenie 12*
Balvenie 15
Balvenie 21*
Blair Athol
Bruichladdich 10
Bruichladdich 15
Glenfarclas 10
Glenfarclas 105
Glenfarclas 21
Glenfarclas 25
Glengoyne 17
Glengoyne 21
Glenkinchie 10
Glenkinchie 1986 DE
Glenlivet 18
Glenlivet 21
Glenmorangie 15
Glenmorangie Sherry
Glenturret 21
Longmorn 15*
Macallan 10
Tomatin 10

Ardbeg 17*
Bowmore 17
Bowmore 21*
Bowmore Dawn*
Bowmore Legend
Bowmore Mariner
Bruichladdich 20
Cragganmore 1984 DE
Glen Garioch 10
Glen Garioch 15*
Glen Garioch 21
Highland Park 12
Laphroaig 10*
Laphroaig 15*
Ledaig
Ledaig 20
Old Pulteney 12
Springbank 10
Tobermory 10

Aberlour 12
Bowmore Darkest
Bunnahabhain 12
Dalmore 12
Dalmore Cigar
Edradour 10
Glendronach 15
Glenfarclas 30
Glenfiddich 15
Glenmorangie Port
Glenrothes 1973
Glen Scotia 14
Highland Park 18*
Highland Park 25*
Macallan 12*
Macallan 25
Macallan 1981
Mortlach 16*
Oban 1980 DE
Scapa 12

Ardbeg 10
Ardbeg 1977
Ardbeg 25 Lord °/he Isles *
Bowmore 12
Caol Ila 15
Clynelish 14
Lagavulin 16
Lagavulin 1979 DE
Laphroaig 10 CS
Ledaig 15
Longrow 10*
Longrow 10 Sherry
Talisker 10*
Talisker 1986 DE

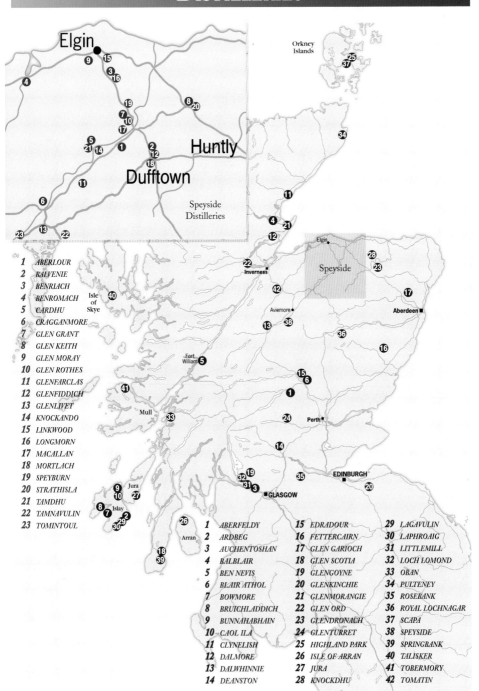

Speyside Distilleries

1 ABERLOUR
2 BALVENIE
3 BENRIACH
4 BENROMACH
5 CARDHU
6 CRAGGANMORE
7 GLEN GRANT
8 GLEN KEITH
9 GLEN MORAY
10 GLEN ROTHES
11 GLENFARCLAS
12 GLENFIDDICH
13 GLENLIVET
14 KNOCKANDO
15 LINKWOOD
16 LONGMORN
17 MACALLAN
18 MORTLACH
19 SPEYBURN
20 STRATHISLA
21 TAMDHU
22 TAMNAVULIN
23 TOMINTOUL

1 ABERFELDY
2 ARDBEG
3 AUCHENTOSHAN
4 BALBLAIR
5 BEN NEVIS
6 BLAIR ATHOL
7 BOWMORE
8 BRUICHLADDICH
9 BUNNAHABHAIN
10 CAOL ILA
11 CLYNELISH
12 DALMORE
13 DALWHINNIE
14 DEANSTON

15 EDRADOUR
16 FETTERCAIRN
17 GLEN GARIOCH
18 GLEN SCOTIA
19 GLENGOYNE
20 GLENKINCHIE
21 GLENMORANGIE
22 GLEN ORD
23 GLENDRONACH
24 GLENTURRET
25 HIGHLAND PARK
26 ISLE OF ARRAN
27 JURA
28 KNOCKDHU

29 LAGAVULIN
30 LAPHROAIG
31 LITTLEMILL
32 LOCH LOMOND
33 OBAN
34 PULTENEY
35 ROSEBANK
36 ROYAL LOCHNAGAR
37 SCAPA
38 SPEYSIDE
39 SPRINGBANK
40 TALISKER
41 TOBERMORY
42 TOMATIN

Producer *Dewar's* **Founded** *1898*

The new 12 year-old bottling from Dewar's is a lightly peated whisky which has not altered much from the Flora & Fauna bottling the previous owners UDV made available. This is despite the fact that the Dewar's expression is three years younger than the 15 year-old Flora & Fauna version. Michael Jackson describes Aberfeldy whisky as being 'best served in its teens' although it is probable that Dewar's discovered the extra three years to be little benefit to the overall style of the whisky.

Using water from the Pittille Burn and two pairs of onion shaped stills most of the whisky made at Aberfeldy goes to blends. It isn't overly apparent the part that Aberfeldy plays in the Dewar's White Label blend but then that isn't surprising considering the number of constituents making up the blend. Aberfeldy is a top class malt whisky and it's not hard to see why the Dewar's had so much success with the distillery.

The distillery, catering to the requests of several different blends, has a good mix of ex-sherry and ex-bourbon casks that are used up to three times. The proportion that goes into the malt whisky is unknown but there are some indicators from the flavours in the whisky that some of the ex-sherry casks see their way into the vatting.

ABERFELDY 12 YEAR-OLD *40%*

Nose	Champagne notes. Appley, nutty and honeyed. Sweet caramel.
Palate	Gentle sweetness with some vanilla. Herbal. Firm body.
Finish	Medium finish with a long sugary aftertaste.
Comment	A lot on offer - An all-round pleasant drink.

Style	C

Region Highlands

Aberfeldy Distillery is now the undisputed home of Dewar's White Label whisky. I say 'now' because for a while it was working itself into insignificance, another beautiful distillery swallowed up in the indecision of an unimaginative company. Now as part of the Bacardi portfolio, Aberfeldy has sprung into life as one of the most visitable distilleries on the planet.

Aberfeldy has always been the spiritual home of Dewar's as John and Tommy Dewar built it in 1896 to ensure a steady supply of malt whisky for their blends. Dewar's White Label Whisky was already a big name and sales were steadily rocketing; becoming the biggest selling blend in the world. Dewar's had been set up exactly fifty years earlier by John Dewar, Tommy and John's father, and the company enjoyed a starring role in the whisky boom of the late 19th Century.

John Dewar stayed in Perth while Tommy became infamous for his marketing techniques travelling around the world. He was an entertaining man and his wit and humour are recorded as 'Dewarisms':

"Competition is the life of trade, but the death of profits."

"No two people are alike, and they are both glad of it."

"Do right and fear no man. Don't write and fear no woman."

"A teetotaller is one who suffers from thirst instead of enjoying it."

The distillery is now a fitting reminder of the genius of the two Dewar's indeed it is nearly impossible to visit Aberfeldy without realising the part Dewar's played in the history of blended whisky. There is now a state-of-the-art visitor's centre that houses a mini-theatre and multi-lingual recorded guides. The emphasis is almost solely on the Dewar's White Label Blend and while this annoys the purists (like myself) who see and drink only single malt whisky it is humbling from time to time to remember that without blends there wouldn't be so much variety.

The distillery was expanded in the 1960's and 1970's under the rule of the DCL. Water is piped from the ruins of Pitilie, a distillery that closed in 1867. The distillery along with Aultmore, Craigellachie and Royal Brackla was sold to Bacardi in 1998 and is situated in beautiful woodland 15 miles off the A9 as you head north from Pitlochry. Adjacent to the distillery is a nature trail where it is possible to see the rare red squirrel (used on the label of the old Flora & Fauna bottling). This coupled with the interactive and hands on nature of the Dewar's World of Whisky Centre based at the distillery, means it is quickly becoming a hot spot of tourist activity.

Producer Chivas Brothers *Founded* 1826

Aberlour (rhymes with hour) is in the top ten of all-time easy-to-drink malt whiskies (perhaps at number one). This makes it a very dangerous whisky as I recall on one occasion sitting on the bank of Loch Lomond with a close friend drinking Aberlour 10 year-old. Let's just say that having concluded our chat swimming in the Loch was not an option. Such is the danger of drinking Aberlour whisky.

With water from the St Dunstan Well and lightly peated malt, the whisky is produced via two pairs of stills and matured in ex-bourbon and ex-sherry casks. It is always medium bodied , full of flavour and always with a hint (or more) of sherry due to the cask policy. The ex-bourbon casks are almost solely sourced from the Wild Turkey Distillery in Kentucky and a majority of the sherry casks are ex-Oloroso sherry matured. Aberlour is bottled in a number of expressions and in the past has had some exclusive bottlings for their main market of France. Aberlour is also marketed heavily towards the Travel Retail shopper (previously Duty Free). This is to give exclusive bottlings to the traveller while annoying the customers who don't travel very often but would still like the expressions!

ABERLOUR 10 YEAR-OLD 40%

Nose	Orange peel. Vanilla fudge. White chocolate.
Palate	Citrusy, more orange peel. Medium bodied - mouth coating.
Finish	Medium finish, sweet and zesty.
Comment	Dangerously drinkable. Each bottle should come with a government warning!
Style	D

ABERLOUR 12 YEAR-OLD SHERRY CASK MATURED 40%

Travel Retail only. Matured exclusively in Oloroso Sherry Casks from Jerez.

Nose	Delicious sweet and fruity sherry notes. Undertones of a tangy maltiness.
Palate	Sweet and dry like a Merlot. Medium bodied.
Finish	Short finish, dry and lingering.
Comment	What a difference a casks makes, a much bolder Aberlour.
Style	F

Region Speyside

ABERLOUR 15 YEAR-OLD DOUBLE CASK MATURED 40%

Travel Retail only. Aged in ex-bourbon and ex-sherry casks.

Nose	Citrus fruits. Slightly sour and appley. Spirity and oaky.
Palate	Sweet oak. Slightly oaky. Medium bodied.
Finish	Long bittersweet finish.
Comment	The nose promises a lot more than is delivered on the palate. Still a very individual dram though.
Style	**B**

ABERLOUR 1990 40%

Travel Retail only. The whisky is 10 years old.

Nose	Unmistakable Aberlour new-make nose. Hint of lychees. Spirity. Malt. Sherry and toffee.
Palate	Medium-to-heavy, slightly oaky. Hints of sherry and malt.
Finish	Medium finish, malty aftertaste.
Comment	Not much differs between the 10 years old and the 1990. (Despite my notes). Still dangerously drinkable however.
Style	**D**

ABERLOUR A' BUNADH 59.6%

Means 'of the origin'. The whisky is between 8 and 10 years old.

Nose	Heavy spices. Cointreau. Mulled wine, stewed fruits.
Palate	Sweet like a liqueur. Oranges and heavy spices.
Finish	Long peppery finish with a dry orange aftertaste.
Comment	Many have claimed thit is the only dram to drink. It isn't hard to see why it moves people to make such statements when drinking it.
Style	**D**

Region speyside

If you blink you'll miss Aberlour Distillery, quietly tucked away in a part of Aberlour that looks as inviting as a graveyard at night. The red and black iron gates also don't help to give the distillery the most promising first glimpse. All of this couldn't be further from the real truth; a distillery that sits in one of the most picturesque parts of Scotland - albeit hidden in the surrounding hills.

Having recently succumbed to what I hope was consumer pressure, Aberlour have built a plush visitors centre and accommodated guides of the distillery (although at the time of writing this is still not open to the public). About time too! Aberlour, thought to mean 'mouth of the chattering burn', sits at the foot of the Ben Rinnes Mountain and takes it's water from the St Dunstan (or Drostan) Well. St Drostan was a travelling missionary with Columcille (St Columbas) and is rumoured to have baptised converts in the local burn.

The real history of Aberlour begins in 1826 when the Laird of Aberlour built the first legal distillery (illegal distilling was rumoured to be taking place long before this). The Laird was to achieve infamy by giving George Smith, the founder of The Glenlivet Distillery, a couple of hair-trigger pistols to keep away angry illicit distillers. Aberlour changed hands once before James Fleming, a local banker, bought the rights to St Drostan's Well and rebuilt the distillery.

Fleming turned the distillery into a success story and coined the phrase 'let the deed show', now the motto of the distillery. Fleming was an unassuming man and tried his hardest to have his philanthropic ways hidden. During his life he designed and built the town hall (later to be named The Fleming Hall) and after his death in 1895 Fleming is still remembered today by the Aberlour Suspension Bridge (also called the 'Penny Brig') and the Fleming Cottage Hospital.

Three years after Fleming's death the distillery suffered a terrible fire which burned down the malt mill, tun room, still house and mash house costing the new owners around £6,000. Thankfully the distillery was insured and was rebuilt to more or less how it appears today. Aberlour continued distilling throughout the Pattison crash of 1898 and despite the brief interruption caused by the two world wars has never ceased to be productive.

Today Aberlour are at the forefront of the new malt drinking culture. Clouding their products in mystique and legend and making several expressions available it is no wonder that France and America, the two largest consumers of whisky, have taken Aberlour to their hearts (or stomachs rather).

Producer *Glenmorangie plc* **Founded** *1815*

Ardbeg is a monster of a malt whisky. It can fill a room with the type of redolence reserved for foods like curries and kebabs. Sitting here writing I have a half-full glass of the potion at arms length and the peat infused pungency is racing up my nostrils. This is not for the squeamish and is definitely an acquired taste.

But the world seems to have acquired it. Sales of Ardbeg have been rocketing as more and more advocates spread the word. Certainly the written works of respected noses such as Jim Murray and Michael Jackson have helped the drink achieve super stardom. And not one to be a party-pooper I have to agree with them. For me though the best version is the softer, more complex 17 year-old that is vatted with some much older and unpeated Ardbeg.

Ardbeg uses malted barley with a higher phenol content than other whisky and sources peaty water from Loch Uigeadail almost a mile from the distillery. The spirit travels through two huge stills, then through a purifier to prevent the heavier spirit being used. It is then left to mature in largely ex-bourbon casks in the distillery's sea facing warehouses.

It will still be several years before we get to see what the new Ardbeg made under the rule of Glenmorangie will be like. If history is anything to go by (and it often is with distilleries), we are in for a treat!

ARDBEG 10 YEAR-OLD 46%

Non chill-filtered.

Nose	Surging scented-sweet peat. Hint of a heather bonfire and a touch of honey.
Palate	Oily and of course immensely peaty. Reaches every corner of the mouth.
Finish	Long finish with wave after wave of peat as an aftertaste.
Comment	A monster of a malt whisky. After the initial numbness and state of shock dies down it is time for the next mouth full. If a whisky could ever make you sweat - this would be it.
Style	G

Region *Islay*

ARDBEG 17 YEAR-OLD 40%

Vatted from a range of Ardbeg expressions including some non-peated.

Nose	Sweet, peaty. Wine Gums. Buttery. Marzipan.
Palate	Perfect balance of sweetness and peat. A light to medium body.
Finish	Bittersweet finish with some toffee.
Comment	This is a superb Ardbeg expression demonstrating beautiful flavour development and harmony.
Style	E

ARDBEG 1977 46%

Non chill-filtered.

Nose	Concentrated seaside. Oily. Tarry. Undertones of currants and a hint of lavender.
Palate	Monstrous peat attacking in uncontrollable waves. Prickly like holly. Medium bodied.
Finish	Long finish that just will not leave the mouth.
Comment	My senses have been taken for ransom. Only one word describes this whisky: 'Attacking'!
Style	G

ARDBEG LORD OF THE ISLES 25 YEAR-OLD 46%

Non chill-filtered.

Nose	Juicy sweet peat. Undertones of oak and currants. Fruit cake. Rum.
Palate peat	Dry peat and brine at first. Medium bodied. Heavy and sweetness surges through as an afterthought.
Finish	Medium, peppery finish. Sweet and lingering aftertaste.
Comment	Edging towards indescribable. You don't have to share this one.
Style	G

Region Islay

The distillery was founded in 1815 by the MacDougalls of Ardbeg who built an unpretentious distillery. It's two pagodas are evidence that Ardbeg used floor maltings right up until 1976, drying the malt in kilns without assistance from fans. This meant that the smoke from the peat was allowed to filter through the malt at a very slow rate - this also meant that the malt had to be turned frequently to prevent stewing.

The distillery came under the control of the Hiram Walker Company in 1979 and was eventually swallowed up by Allied Distillers having taken over Hiram Walker. This, as seems to be the case for any promising malt distillery under the control of Allied Distillers, spelled disaster for Ardbeg. Allied, in all their wisdom, could not see the future for malt whisky and began experimenting with the peating levels of the whisky. This was to try and find a more agreeable balance in the whisky so that it could fit into the recipes of their blends such as Teachers. However, I have to take time to thank them for their experiments as otherwise the wonderful vatting that is the 17 year-old would not be available.

Ardbeg insists on maturing all of its whisky on site and uses age-old methods of warehousing. The current warehouse staff are among the finest gentlemen you are ever likely to meet and if given the chance, enjoy watching 'Yogi' and 'Dugga' stowing the barrels carefully one at a time. This part of the making of whisky has changed the least since its conception over a hundred years ago.

Now, in its current guise, Ardbeg is enjoying a fresh revival from a fabulous distilling pedigree. Glenmorangie, having purchased the distillery and maturing stocks, have breathed life into what used to be a desolate place. The stills are firing once again and the new visitors centre, shop and cafe only adds to the admiration most imbibers already have for the whisky.

Producer *Arran Distillers* **Founded** *1995*

With Arran Distillery being just six years old it is difficult to say how good the whisky is going to be in five or seven years. However, a couple expressions of the Arran malt and the Lochranza blend have been made available and signs look good. The 5 year-old has a young, appley taste to it that is quite delicious and requires much further inspection. As is the case with all young whisky however, the vatting may change and future Arran whisky may bare no resemblance to the current expression. I hope that the future of Arran follows through on all of the promises from it now.

An unpeated malt, Arran sources its water from the Eason Bioroch Burn from the hills just behind the distillery. It currently has two fairly small stills and uses a mix of 30% ex-bourbon and 70% ex-sherry casks.

ARRAN **43%**

This whisky is no more than 5 years old.

Nose	Fresh, new-make. Apples and un-ripe pears. Icing sugar. Sharp.
Palate	Cooking apples, icing sugar. Vanilla. Quite light.
Finish	Short, bittersweet finish.
Comment	Already a terrific whisky. Hopefully the next few years will improve Arran as it matures - if that is possible.
Style	A

Region *Islands*

It's not all doom and gloom for the whisky industry. Passions run high in certain circles so much so that distilleries have been bought, replenished, restored, put back to work and even built. Most exciting for writers, drinkers and anyone with any interest in Scotch is the creation of a brand new distillery. Only four have been built in Scotland over the last eleven years; Kininvie, Speyside, Isle of Arran and Kilchoman (and in that order).

The first mash started on 24th June 1995 and was run for one week to commission the plant. Thereafter the plant was shut down again to allow building to be completed. It was then re-started on 1st August 1995, when production commenced. The brainchild of Harold Currie the ex Managing Director of Chivas, it was a long time in coming and a project that sent him in every direction before choosing the most southerly of the western isles.

Arran lies below the Highland line to the east of the Kintyre Peninsula. No doubt the area was previously overshadowed by the reputation of the Isle of Islay and Campbeltown whiskies. Arran was at one time reported to make the best whisky in Scotland and it was this reputation that led Harold Currie to consider the small island for the site of his distillery. After ruling out Lagg (which had been the site of a previous distillery) due to contaminated water, Currie decided on the relatively isolated area of Lochranza.

Construction of the squat, pagoda-roofed distillery was not problem-free however. With the discovery of a pair of golden eagles nesting on Creag Dhubh, the hill southeast of the distillery, work had to cease to allow the birds to settle in. This was not the last time that a rarity was spotted near the distillery, as HRH Queen Elizabeth II was available to open the new visitor's centre in 1997 when she visited the island on the final tour of the Royal Yacht Britannia.

The distillery was forced into finding funding, as distilleries have to wait a long time before seeing returns on their investments. Bonds were sold as production began and after three years (1998) the company distributed the Lochranza blend to their shareholders. Not a bad idea if you ask me. Give or take a dishonest dealer here and there the distillery has done remarkably well and is embracing the new malt drinking market with open arms. Harold Currie has achieved what most of us can only dream about, his own distillery!

Producer *Morrison Bowmore Distillers* **Founded** *1823*

Auchentoshan (Ock en tosh en) is not afraid to represent the true Lowland style using its three stills for triple distillation. It is totally unpeated with no peat in its water source, the Cochna Loch in the Old Kilpatrick Hills. This makes it a lighter elegant whisky. The Auchentoshan Three Wood has flavour characteristics similar to Bushmills, and although that may insult either distillery it is the best expression of Auchentoshan and is simply so full of flavour that I couldn't fathom buying any other expression of Auchentoshan.

Some have claimed that Auchentoshan is an excellent starter whisky for the uninitiated in the whisky world. I find that a little insulting to Auchentoshan after all how many malt drinkers were introduced to single malt whisky through Lagavulin? Auchentoshan does present a range of whiskies to suit almost any occasion. Where it has omissions, its sister distilleries Glen Garioch and Bowmore certainly fill in the spaces.

AUCHENTOSHAN SELECT 40%

Made from whisky between 8-10 years old.

Nose	Grainy. New-make. Scented, sherry, cooked rice. Quite fresh.
Palate	Starchy, bitter - very light. Light body.
Finish	Long, dry and oaky finish.
Comment	A light aperitif perhaps.
Style	A

AUCHENTOSHAN 10 YEAR-OLD 40%

Nose	Sugary, herbal. Flowers. Caramel chocolate, heather.
Palate	Gentle. A beer-bitter taste. Light body.
Finish	Warming, medium finish.
Comment	Demonstrating the Lowland stereotypical softness.
Style	A

Region *Lowlands*

AUCHENTOSHAN 21 YEAR-OLD 43%

Nose	Immediate oakiness, followed by sweet wine notes. Perfumed and delicate. Buttery.
Palate	Delicate and soft. Little sweetness which is a surprise. Tongue coating but not oily.
Finish	An incredibly long finish. Just a hint of oakiness that comes as an afterthought long after you have put your glass down.
Comment	Another superb expression.
Style	C

AUCHENTOSHAN THREE WOOD 43%

Aged for at least ten years in ex-bourbon oak until being finished in Oloroso casks and then Pedro Ximenez casks.

Nose	Delicious combinations of fruit and sherry. Malty, full flavoured with spices and orange.
Palate	Superb sweetness, sharp and salty. Medium body.
Finish	Medium sweet. Delicate.
Comment	By far the best expression of Auchentoshan. Similar on the nose and palate to an Irish whiskey. Shouldn't come as a surprise though!
Style	D

Region Lowlands

The most traditional of Lowland malts takes its water from just above the Highland line in the Kilpatrick Hills. This begs the question 'what makes a Lowland malt?' Unfortunately there is no answer to this question. I will look at Glenkinchie later but with regard to Auchentoshan it is the unique method of triple distillation that defines it as a Lowland malt whisky. Auchentoshan uses three different stills for distillation utilising an intermediate still to separate strong alcohol and strong feints from the low wines before it is distilled for the last time and then laid to rest.

Auchentoshan enjoys a high profile as one of the few remaining Lowland malts. Built at the turn of the nineteenth century the distillery changed hands many times before Tennents (and later Bass) bought the distillery. Situated just ten miles outside of Glasgow, the whitewashed walls of the distillery look a little out of place surrounded by brick flats and houses in the Clydebank area. Auchentoshan has led a charmed life and has always been sought after by blenders and consumers of single malts (it was one of the first distilleries to be bottled as a single malt).

Auchentoshan was bought by the Eadie Cairns company in 1969 and was completely re-equipped bringing the potential output of the distillery to one million gallons a year.

The distillery has had a fairly long run of having only one competitor for the spot of greatest working Lowland malt. However, Glenkinchie, the other Lowland malt, would be more at home in the Northern Highlands and so it is the revival of Bladnoch that threatens Auchentoshan's near monopoly over blenders and consumers of the southerly malts. Will this inspire Morrison Bowmore to share the marketing a little more fairly between its malt whiskies? As with all new ventures, experiments and projects in the whisky industry only time will tell.

Producer Inver House Distillers **Founded** *1790*

Whether you are drinking Balblair Elements or the 16 year-old expression it is difficult to put down your glass or not refill it once emptied. Perhaps a bit lighter than you would expect from the area, with similar flavour characteristics as its neighbour Glenmorangie but so well balanced to make it one of the most agreeable malts available.

This is an unpeated malt although considerable peat can be found in its water sourced from the Allt Dearg Burn. Using two fairly large short necked pot stills, and a mix of ex-bourbon and ex-sherry butts, the whisky is left to mature in their traditional damp earth floored dunnage warehouses.

The whisky, as I have already mentioned is incredibly well balanced reminding me of some of the Japanese whiskies (or should that be the other way round). The light peat and sweetness of the malt allows the drinker to let the taste, rather than the nose, do the talking. This is not the greatest all-rounder in the whisky world but it is certainly one of the most delightful drams.

BALBLAIR ELEMENTS 40%

The whisky is from 8 - 10 years old.

Nose	Lots of honey and heather. A coffee-cream nose with bitter chocolate.
Palate	A sweet, creamy palate with soft, dry peat.
Finish	A short, icing-sugar finish.
Comment	Not a patch on the 16 year old but delightful none the less. A very reasonable whisky considering the price.
Style	**D**

BALBLAIR 16 YEAR-OLD 40%

Nose	Tangerines. Creamy vanilla. Marzipan. Undertones of sherry and spice.
Palate	Creamy-silky smooth, almost like a cream liqueur. Light - medium body.
Finish	A soft, smoky finish.
Comment	A beautifully balanced whisky. Surging sweet, creamy notes on the nose and a delicious soft and creamy palate. A cracker!
Style	**D**

Region *Highlands*

The history of the distillery in its current location dates from around the 1860's although distilling in the area dates back to 1790 and even earlier if you take into account the illicit distillers. Tain was very suitable for the illicit distillers on account of the unlimited peat and excellent water. It is no surprise that this small area of Scotland produces some of the greatest whiskies in Scotland and Scotland's favourite whisky.

Balblair, meaning 'village in the plain', is very much a traditional distillery and has gone relatively unchanged from its original construction. Balblair had the longest bonded warehouse in Scotland until fire regulations meant that a dividing wall was erected. All of the warehouses have earth floors except for Warehouse No.3 which was commandeered during WW2 and a concrete floor put in to accommodate a canteen!

The distillery suffered a long period of inactivity from 1915 to 1947 until Robert Cumming, a solicitor from Banff, bought it. Cumming set about expanding Balblair and it was at this time that the stills became steam heated.

In 1970 Cumming retired and the distillery seemed doomed to never reap its just rewards until Inver House Distillers bought it from Allied Distillers in 1996. Now under the policy of Inver House who produce other great whiskies such as Old Pulteney and Speyburn, Balblair is enjoying a period of revival and market penetration. The floor maltings were closed in 1975 and the old malt barn was, as seems traditional, turned into a hospitality suite for entertaining visitors.

Producer William Grant & Sons Founded 1892

Balvenie is the most honeyed whisky there is, and the older it gets the better it gets. The sweet fruitiness that emerges (as is the case in old Glenfiddich expressions) is most delightful.

Balvenie is one of only a few distilleries to still operate their own maltings, although the malt is only lightly peated. Like Glenfiddich its sister company, it uses water from the Robbie Dhu Springs in the Conval Hills behind the distillery. The spirit then passes through two of nine stills and is allowed to sleep in ex-bourbon, ex-sherry or ex-port casks.

The popular choice is The Balvenie 12 year-old DoubleWood (not to be thought of as a double malt as there is no such thing). My choice is the 21 year-old Portwood, but only because I have a preference for port wood finishes. Whichever is your preference there really isn't a bad Balvenie. A distillery blessed with a Midas touch perhaps.

BALVENIE 10 YEAR-OLD FOUNDERS RESERVE 43%

This is the standard bottling.

Nose	Wave after wave of delicious spicy honey. Nutmeg. Cinnamon. Malty.
Palate	Smooth, medium body. Quite oily and fat. Creamy and malty.
Finish	A long honey, oaky finish.
Comment	One of the best 10 year-old whiskies from Speyside.
Style	C

BALVENIE 15 YEAR-OLD 50.4%

This is a single cask bottling.

Nose	Sweet oak, spicy, citrusy. Fruitcake and cinnamon.
Palate	Chewy, sweet oak and extraordinary waves of honey. So much honey.
Finish	A long, honey aftertaste.
Comment	You could say too much honey and you would be right. But damn it if it doesn't taste good!
Style	D

Region *Speyside*

BALVENIE PORT WOOD 21 YEAR-OLD *40%*

Finished for 6-12 months in port pipes.

Nose   Tangerines, sherry. Sweet oak. Fruity and slightly minty.

Palate   Sweet oak and appley. Medium body. Fruity.

Finish   A medium finish. Sweet with a tangerine aftertaste.

Comment   Glorious whisky. Wonderful sweet oak and fruit. Love the tangerines!

Style   D

BALVENIE DOUBLEWOOD 12 YEAR-OLD *43%*

Matured first in ex-bourbon barrels and then in first fill ex-sherry casks.

Nose   Sherry, malt. Rich honey - masses of it. Fruitcake, slightly spicy.

Palate   Full-on honey sweetness. Not as round as the 10 year-old. Medium bodied and spicy.

Finish   Medium finish. Honey sweet.

Comment   It is obvious why this is the popular choice.
              Much more fruit and honey than the 10 year-old.

Style   D

Region Speyside

Very little is known about what makes whisky taste the way it does. Despite extensive research into the chemistry of the process we still know very little about why whisky tastes and, more importantly, smells the way it does. Scientists have been able to identify certain flavours that are created in certain parts of the process. They have also been able to better understand some of the chemical reactions that occur between the whisky and the copper stills and between the whisky and the oak casks.

Yet, with all their white-coat brilliance scientists still cannot explain how two distilleries built on the same land using the same water and the same barley produce completely different whiskies. Granted that in this case the whiskies aren't chalk and cheese but they are a long way from being two peas in a pod!

Glenfiddich was the first distillery to be built by William Grant on the outskirts of Dufftown and in 1892 on the success of Glenfiddich he built Balvenie six years later literally next door. The first spirit running from the stills in 1893. Balvenie and Kininvie (the third distillery to be built on the same estate) are not as picturesque as Glenfiddich, and it is easy to see that many more visitors are received in the cute little courtyard of Glenfiddich than the more workman-like looking Balvenie.

Balvenie is not to be missed though as it contains one of the few remaining floor maltings and kilns that produces a little less than 10% of the malted barley required for distillation. The distillery has never changed hands and is still owned by William Grant & Sons.

Whereas Glenfiddich was built with spare parts from Cardhu Distillery, Balvenie was equipped with stills from the Lagavulin and Glen Albyn Distilleries. Whatever William Grant intended, the new spirit must have taken everyone by surprise.

Producer Nikka Distilling Company *Founded* 1825

Ben Nevis is predominantly used for blending and even has its own blend Dew of Ben Nevis, which was also the name given to its first release.

A medium peated whisky using water from the Allt a Mhuillin Burn which flows from two lochans 3,000ft up Ben Nevis. Ben Nevis has four large stills and matures the spirit in ex-bourbon, ex-sherry and ex-French wine casks.

There is huge potential for this isolated distillery to take a larger share of the single malt market. The current 10 year-old has a lot to offer and recent awards and exclamations of delight have not been misguided. One for the marketers!

BEN NEVIS 10 YEAR-OLD 46%

Nose	Immediate scent of pine nuts. Malty sweetness. Yeasty. Cooked dough.
Palate	A mouthful of bittersweet bread and nut flavours.
Finish	Short finish but very pleasant.
Comment	A very individual dram. Reminds me of marmite and like marmite you either love it or hate it. I love it!
Style	B

Region Highlands

Ben Nevis Distillery sits at the foot of the highest mountain in Scotland (1,344m/4,406ft), which bears the same name. Perhaps because of this scenery visitors are expecting an equally splendid distillery to match. Unfortunately Ben Nevis is not the cute little distillery, hidden away in a glen that some might romantically imagine. Nevertheless it is a frequently visited distillery due to its location in Fort William.

'Long John' McDonald who acquired his name by being rather tall, built the distillery in 1825. Although Long John's association with the distillery was short the name remains associated through the blend called Long John. In 1878 a second distilling unit was built nearby and was simply called Nevis. This was an extension built to keep up with demand in the late 19th Century whisky boom. This second site operated for thirty years before being absorbed into the Ben Nevis distillery in 1908.

The distillery remained in the hands of McDonalds and Macdonnells until 1955 when a Mr Joseph Hobbs bought the distillery on returning to Scotland having made a fortune in Canada. The Long John Co had been sold in 1920 and so the distillery became the Ben Nevis Distillery Company Ltd. While Hobbs was in charge a Coffey still was installed to accommodate Hobbs ideas for blending. The still lasted until 1981 when Long John Distillers bought back the distillery and returned the distillery to 100% malt distilling.

The distillery was closed five years later and then reopened in 1990 having been bought from Whitbread (who had taken over Long John Distillers) by Nikka Distillers of Japan. Under their rule the distillery has been able to bottle many different expressions of Ben Nevis and many specialty one-off bottlings have also been released onto the market.

Producer *Chivas Brothers* **Founded** *1898*

B enriach uses the same water supply as its neighbouring sister distillery Longmorn, the Burnside Springs, it uses the same unpeated malt and similarly use ex-bourbon and ex-sherry casks. Despite this the two whiskies are very different with Benriach being considerably lighter. This may be due to Benriach's stills being larger, although by no means would they be considered huge. It would also be safe to conclude that a greater amount of ex-bourbon casks are used to produce Benriach.

Most of the whisky produced at Benriach goes for blending and previous owners Seagrams have recently discontinued the current 10 year-old bottling. Hopefully new owners Pernod Ricard will release a new more dynamic bottling.

BENRIACH 10 YEAR-OLD 43%

Nose	Malty, spirity. Perfume. Spiky. Oaky.
Palate	Sweet, very oaky. Quite light.
Finish	Medium finish. Sweet.
Comment	Not much to Benriach. Fairly pleasant to drink but not much on the nose.
Style	A

Region *Speyside*

A distillery whose future looks uncertain after the sale by Seagram Distillers is Benriach Distillery. Built in response to the great whisky boom of the late 19th Century by John Duff, Benriach has lost out in terms of fame to its neighbour Longmorn. Benriach shares one of those odd situations taking the same water, barley and peat as its neighbouring distillery and yet making a completely different whisky. Benriach has smaller stills than Longmorn and yet makes a lighter whisky.

Both Longmorn and Benriach were built at the same time although Longmorn started distilling first and Benriach continued shortly afterwards. Duff could not have foreseen the great Pattison Crash and Benriach only enjoyed two years of distilling before closing down at the turn of the 20th Century. The distillery was closed for a further 65 years returning from obscurity as part of The Glenlivet Distillers portfolio. Throughout its closure Benriach operated its floor maltings although it was unable to keep up with demand and supplied only a small percentage of the malt required.

Seagram's took over The Glenlivet Distillers in 1977 and was in turn sold to Pernod Ricard in 2001. Pernod Ricard have an excellent history of restoring and looking after the great whisky distilleries. But with Longmorn immediately next door making a heavier and more sought after whisky, the new owners have their work cut out for them in restoring a charming distillery that is still capable of producing traditionally made malt from it's own floor maltings.

Producer Gordon & MacPhail **Founded** 1898

Benromach is an extraordinary distillery to visit as almost all of the distilling process is carried out under one roof. The stills were removed by UDV who had let the distillery go silent and new owners Gordon & MacPhail replaced them with smaller stills hopefully to give a heavier spirit. This, I hope, will give Benromach more character as the Benromach that we drink today, and for the next 7 - 10 years will be that made under the rule of UDV.

The new whisky is made with a lightly peated malt, and spring water from the Romach Hills. Two stills are used for distillation with maturation being in ex-bourbon and ex-sherry casks. Based on their history of purchasing casks from a great variety of distilleries, Gordon & MacPhail believe a better product is achieved with the traditional malting floor method. They are therefore very stringent with the peating levels of the malted barley, striving to reproduce the characteristics achieved by the traditional method through the modern drum malting process.

Now being independently run there is a much more concerted effort to secure the best materials for the process and to ensure that the spirit that is made is not a filler for blends as was its previous role. Perhaps now Gordon & MacPhail can really show what the distillery is capable of.

BENROMACH 18 YEAR-OLD 40%

Nose   Soft Fruits, Icing Sugar. Blackberries. Slight hint of spiciness. Prickly.

Palate   Again quite soft. Some delicate fruitiness and caramel.

Finish   A hint oak sets up a delicate finish.

Comment   Has aged gracefully retaining much of it's charm.

Style   C

Region speyside

B enromach was built in 1898 by Mr McCallum the owner of Glen Nevis Distillery in Campbeltown and F Brickman a spirit dealer in Leith. The distillery was opened in 1900 but closed immediately probably due to the economic collapse in the whisky industry. The distillery was operated on and off until 1938 when it was bought by Train & McKintyre a subsidiary of Associated Scottish Distilleries who in turn was owned by the National Distillers of America. Train & McIntyre was bought by the DCL in 1953 and subsequently rebuilt in 1966.

Benromach was closed in 1983 and then acquired in 1993 by Gordon & MacPhail, the largest independent bottler of whisky in the world. Suitably Benromach sits down the road from the Gordon & MacPhail head offices in Elgin. HRH Prince Charles officially opened the distillery in 1998, a century after it was built on the River Findhorn in Forres.

Gordon & MacPhail had previously enjoyed the role as primarily the sole bottler and distributor of single malts. Much credit is given to the small family company for the revival of single malt whisky. Indeed many distilleries' whisky would never see the back of a single malt label had it not been for the foresight of previous generations of Urquhart's, Gordon's and MacPhail's.

Producer UDV Founded 1798

Very little Blair Athol whisky is bottled as a single malt. In fact you are far more likely to find an independent bottler's expression of Blair Athol than you are to find the 12 year-old Flora & Fauna bottled by UDV. This seems to be the case with most distilleries that are appointed the home of big named blends. The simple explanation is that blends keep the whisky industry alive and without them there would be very little single malt whisky available.

Blair Athol is made with lightly peated malt, water from the Alt na Dour burn and distilled via two pairs of stills.

When I first tried Blair Athol I was amazed how fruity it was and it isn't hard to see the part it plays at the heart of the Bell's blend. Certainly Arthur Bell & Sons knew what they were doing when they invested sixteen years into the development of the distillery.

The independent bottlings that are more commonly available of Blair Athol quite often show a maltier character to Blair Athol, as they tend to be bottled from ex-bourbon casks. Do not be deceived by their apparent lack of colour as colour does not always mean tasty.

BLAIR ATHOL 12 YEAR-OLD 43%

Nose	Stewed fruits. New-make. Cider. Cinnamon rolls.
Palate	Incredibly fruity. Oaky and earthy. Sugared raisins. Medium bodied.
Finish	Quite dry and fruity. Medium finish.
Comment	As the heart of Bell's, Blair Athol gives some depth and fruit. Deserves more attention as a single malt.
Style	**D**

Region Highlands

Finding Blair Athol Distillery is not the simplest task to undertake. Driving north on the A9 from Perth any logical traveller would turn off at Blair Atholl having passed Pitlochry seven miles to the south. Sadly the traveller having discovered the exact location of the distillery has no choice but to turn around and head back. From experience I can tell you that it is not as annoying as it sounds.

Currently Blair Athol is home to Bell's blended whisky although the association with Arthur Bell & Sons did not occur until 1933 by which time both Bell's and Blair Athol were well established. It is believed that the original distillery built in 1798 was called Aldour and was built during the great boom period of the late 18th Century by Stewart & Robertson. The distillery then changed hands a number of times before Arthur Bell & Sons took an interest.

Blair Athol was silent from 1932 until 1949 meaning that Bell's had to wait sixteen years before seeing results from their purchase. The distillery was also rebuilt in 1949 which added to the delay. The distillery was expanded from two stills to four in 1973 and had a dark grains plant added two years later.

Recently the distillery has benefited from a plush visitors centre that helps keep Blair Athol one of the most visited distilleries in Scotland. Something to note on visiting the distillery are the black trees surrounding the warehouses. This is common around most warehouses (if there are trees) and is attributed to a fungus that thrives on the high alcoholic vapours from the maturing casks. This does not harm the trees however.

Producer Morrison Bowmore Distillers **Founded** 1779

Bowmore is such a consistently good whisky that like Aberlour it is a bit dangerous. There is a tradition that any bottle of Bowmore opened has the cork thrown away immediately. This is more of a problem than a tradition because Bowmore is so drinkable that often the cork does not get replaced soon enough and the next time you reach for the bottle it is empty.

This isn't a complaint, rather a compliment to the skill and craftsmanship of Bowmore Distillers who get it right almost always. Using a good mixture of ex-sherry and ex-bourbon barrels, Bowmore are able to bottle a number of expressions including some heavier expressions (Bowmore Darkest, Bowmore Black) and some lighter, although peatier expressions (Bowmore Surf, Bowmore Legend). All-in-all approach with caution, but definitely approach!

Currently the distillery takes its water from the peat rich River Laggan and the peat for the kilns is also cut locally. Bowmore, like Laphroaig still use traditional floor maltings that account for a third of their malt. The kilning process is unique at Bowmore as it was at Glen Garioch where peat is crumbled and moistened allowing more smoke to infuse through the malt. This process allows the distillery to use around 80% less peat than before. The kilns are also air blown rather than open fired.

Bowmore has four onion shaped stills and utilises a variety of casks including sherry, claret and port wood. Some of the casks are then left to mature in a vault which is partly below sea level at high tide.

BOWMORE LEGEND 40%

The whisky is 8-10 years old.

Nose	Smoky and very malty. Worts. Shades of icing sugar.
Palate	Round. Sweet, smoky. Medium body.
Finish	Medium, sweet, then peaty finish.
Comment	This expression captures all of the smells from within a distillery in one bottle!
Style	E

Region Islay

BOWMORE 12 YEAR-OLD 40%

Nose	Smoky peat. Bonfire. Undertones of sweet oak.
Palate	Spiky. Peaty. Fireworks in the mouth. Medium bodied.
Finish	Medium finish. Long bittersweet aftertaste.
Comment	Wonderful explosions of peat on the tongue and a delicious bonfire nose.

Style G

BOWMORE MARINER 15 YEAR-OLD 43%

Nose	Deliciously minty and fresh. Sweet peat. Fragrant. Peat.
Palate	Mint humbugs. Fresh. Medium-to-heavy body.
Finish	Long, intriguing finish. Sweet aftertaste.
Comment	Another excellent whisky that won't allow you to put the glass down.

Style E

BOWMORE DARKEST 43%

Aged in ex-bourbon casks with final maturation period in Oloroso butts.

Nose	Rich sherry and peat smoke. Background bonfire notes. Stewed fruits.
Palate	Full on dry sherry being washed out by peat. Heavy and very rich. Salty.
Finish	Medium finish. Lots of sherry.
Comment	A real after dinner whisky. Very rich.

Style F

BOWMORE DAWN 51.5%

Aged in ex-bourbon casks with final maturation period in Ruby Port pipes.

Nose	Icing sugar. Minty, herbal. Refreshing sea breeze. Fresh soft fruits.
Palate	Immense sweet peat. Minty. Medium body. Herbal.
Finish	Long, spiky finish. Very fresh.
Comment	Bowmore once again demonstrate their excellence. Utterly delicious.

Style E

Region Islay

BOWMORE 17 YEAR-OLD 43%

Nose	Minty, spirity. Soft delicate peat. Fruity.
Palate	Minty, fresh. Sweet peat. Medium body.
Finish	Short finish, earthy, peaty.
Comment	Is Bowmore trying to copy Glen Garioch or vice versa? Either way it makes for a stunning dram.

Style   E

BOWMORE 21 YEAR-OLD 43%

Nose	Sour fruits, apples & pears. Fresh. Sugary, oaky, fruit pastilles and a hint of smoke.
Palate	Fruit, fresh, minty, bitter (but not unpleasant).
Finish	Long finish, licorice aftertaste.
Comment	Spectacular, superb, wonderful, extraordinary, incredible… need I go on?

Style   E

Region Islay

The oldest distillery on Islay, built in 1779, Bowmore is appropriately in the capital of Islay. The town of Bowmore was moved from Bridgend in the late 1760's by the laird, Daniel Campbell and the distillery was built and still lies at the bottom of the main street that runs through the town. Despite this the two tall necked pagodas are prominent from any angle. It is impossible to visit Bowmore without noticing the round church sitting on top of the hill. It is rumoured to have been built round so that there were no corners for the devil to hide in. Perhaps however, the builders just liked the idea of a round church - we shall never know!

Bowmore Distillery, having been built by David Simpson, remained in the family until 1837 when it was bought by the Mutters of Glasgow. Under their reign, a programme of expansion and renovation was undertaken. The distillery was later sold to a consortium from London until J B Sherriff & Co took over in 1925. Sherriff's went bust and Stanley P Morrison bought the distillery in 1963 and expanded it further. Suntory of Japan now owns Morrison Bowmore - thankfully though, their management policy seems to be one of 'left to run on your own'. This Bowmore do with brilliance and flair.

Bowmore Distillery and the whisky are both slightly overshadowed by stories of the employees, whether past or present. Most books will tell you about the incredible cooper Davy Bell who started work in 1919 retired in 1970 having been Scotland's most senior cooper for the last eight years of his employment.

Then there is Christine Logan the distillery shop manager. Her passion for the distillery she works for and the island she lives on makes you feel that you belong to her small part of Scotland. It is testament to Islay and Bowmore that the company has continually employed staff that are excellent ambassadors for their whisky. Oh, and the whisky is pretty good as well.

Producer Bruichladdich Distillery   **Founded** *1881*

Although Bruichladdich (Brew ick laddie) is the most westerly working distillery in Scotland, it is protected somewhat from the raw elements of the Atlantic Ocean by a range of hills. Bruichladdich uses spring water, which has a high peat content and operates four tall-necked pot stills. It has been considered the gentler of the Islay malts for some time, that was until the traditionalists got their hands on the distillery and changed the finished product. Those of you who reach for their new bottle of Bruichladdich expecting a gentle sea breeze will be a little taken back but not disappointed. You will find the new batch, vatted under the scrutiny of Jim McEwan, to be quite an accomplished dram.

What is being made for the future however is more intriguing. Like Springbank, Bruichladdich plans to make a mixture of heavily peated and lightly peated whisky. It will be a new decade before we see the results but I guarantee that due to the care and attention that has already been invested we are on the verge of something special.

All Bruichladdich expressions are un chill-filtered which although it can give a cloudy appearance when cold or mixed with water, results in more flavours being retained.

BRUICHLADDICH 10 YEAR-OLD 46%

Nose	Sweet malt. Dry peat. Bag of sweets. Honey and cloves. Herbal. Fudge.
Palate	Orangey-sweet. Medium body. Slightly peaty. Dry
Finish	Long. Lots of licorice. Sweet and utterly delicious.
Comment	A complete upheaval from previous Bruichladdich. Sumptuous.
Style	**D**

Region Islay

BRUICHLADDICH 15 YEAR-OLD 46%

Nose	Slightly spiky. Sweet fresh peat. Scented. Currants. Bready. Green.
Palate	Fruity sweetness. Spiky peat. Bready. Medium-heavy body.
Finish	Acres long. Smoky finish. Warming.
Comment	A lot going on, making it an outstanding dram.
Style	D

BRUICHLADDICH 20 YEAR-OLD 46%

Nose	Peach skin. Creamy. Lemon meringue. Tiniest hint of smoke. Minty.
Palate	Slightly malty. Creamy and surprisingly soft. Medium bodied. Spiky sweetness
Finish	Medium peppery finish that lingers elegantly.
Comment	Delicious nose totally unexpected with some completely individual flavours.
Style	E

Region Islay

Bruichladdich was built in 1881 by three Harvey brothers who also owned the Yoker and Dundashill distilleries in Glasgow. At the time, Dundashill was the largest malt distillery in Scotland. Bruichladdich was to benefit from a revolutionary building material called concrete that had been patented by John MacDonald of Glasgow. Thus Bruichladdich Distillery is slightly different in appearance from its peers on the Isle of Islay. Bruichladdich is also the only distillery on Islay not to be built directly next to the sea being separated by a small coastal road.

Bruichladdich stands on the opposite shore to Bowmore on the western shore of Loch Indaal. There was previously a distillery called Loch Indaal (or Lochindaal) situated in Port Charlotte a few miles south of Bruichladdich. Bottles of Lochindaal can be found lurking on store shelves but do not get excited thinking you have found a rare bottling of a long-lost distillery. Lochindaal closed in 1929 and the bottles that now bear the name are spuriously titled and contain Bruichladdich whisky.

The distillery changed hands a number of times and at one point was owned by Invergordon Distillers who expanded the distillery. Eventually the distillery came under the ownership of JBB who kept the distillery working seasonally to retain stock and to experiment with peating levels in the barley. The distillery remained with JBB until 2001 when Murray McDavid bought it with a consortium of financiers including owners of La Reserve Wine and also the ex-Brand Ambassador of Bowmore, Jim McEwan.

Under the new management Bruichladdich is being restored to full working capacity and the old bottlings of Bruichladdich are being replaced using the stock that was bought as part of the deal with JBB. Some of the stock is peated and thus Bruichladdich could change its image as a gentle island malt. What is certain is that Bruichladdich will come out from the shadow of all the giant whiskies on Islay and will begin to attract visitors from all over the world. The distillery is to incorporate facilities for major functions, tastings and seminars. With Jim McEwan in the driving seat people will come from miles to attend, of that I am certain!

Producer *The Edrington Group* **Founded** *1881*

Bunnahabhain (Boon a hav en) is quite an oily, heavy whisky and is used in blends such as Cutty Sark and Black Bottle. It is unknown when the distillery began using non-peated malt but it does present a little insight into what the whiskies of the southern distilleries of Islay might taste like without their peat.

Bunnahabhain has never enjoyed a high profile despite being owned by The Edrington Group who look after their malts very well. This is probably due to Highland Park being the preferred island malt in their portfolio. This also means that Bunnahabhain is only bottled as the 12 year-old (other than the odd commemorative bottling). Perhaps with it being such an oily malt a younger expression may show a lighter side to the whisky.

An upeated malt, Bunnahabhain's water is sourced from the Margadale Spring and is piped to the distillery to avoid running it over the mossy and peaty land. Never the less, peat still has a small influence on the water. The distillery uses ex-bourbon and ex-sherry casks, both of which are evident in the whisky, all be it slight. Four huge onion shaped stills are in use although they are by no means utilised to capacity.

BUNNAHABHAIN *12 YEAR-OLD 40%*

Nose	Rich oak and sherry. A hint of spiciness and slightly earthy.
Palate	Bitter, but very pleasant. Sherry and oak. Very viscose.
Finish	Finishes like a Belgian Kriek beer. Quite prickly.
Comment	A peculiar dram with a lot to keep it interesting.
Style	F

Region *Islay*

Jim Murray once wrote an excellent article on the effects of tasting whisky at the source of creation. He alluded to the fact that once you got home the charms, smells and hypnotic effect of the distillery would often wear off and the dram might only be a glimpse of what it has previously tasted like. I did not completely understand what he meant until I drank Bunnahabhain, sitting at the end of the pier, staring into the sea and the Isle of Jura in the distance. It was a magical moment and made me feel that Bunnahabhain was the greatest liquid ever to have passed my lips.

On returning to the mainland I immediately bought a bottle of Bunnahabhain 12 year old and was utterly dismayed to find it did not bottle the magic that was tasted at the distillery. I am convinced to this day that distillery managers add a little magic dust to each dram given on site just to make you go and buy more!

Bunnahabhain is the most northerly of the Islay distilleries sitting on a bay that is almost out of eyesight until you are upon it. The drive to the distillery takes you up and down and around and how the big juggernaut lorries manage to navigate the windy road is testament to their driving ability.

In 1881, in a relatively inhospitable part of Islay, Bunnahabhain was established together with a small supporting community, but its remoteness caused headaches for the contractors from the start. Not only did the distillery have to be built but houses, schoolrooms, a pier and the road to Port Askaig. All of this still remains despite a hurricane that blew two large steam boilers from Islay to Jura! In the same year Bruichladdich was also founded making them the youngest surviving distilleries on Islay.

Islay is not the easiest island to navigate around by boat and there have been over 250-recorded wrecks. The most evident is an ocean-going trawler that has rusted for 27 years only a few hundred yards away from the distillery.

On visiting Bunnahabhain you must walk to the end of the pier with a large glass of Bunnahabhain 12 years old, just when the sun is about to set. This will allow all the magic to enter the glass and make you feel as if there couldn't be a better drink on the planet.

Producer UDV Founded 1846

Caol Ila (Cull Eela) is overshadowed by its sister distillery Lagavulin. This is in most respects warranted as Lagavulin has always been a popular malt and has by far the prettier distillery, not to mention more accessible (just). But comparing Caol Ila to Lagavulin is akin to comparing a foot and a hand. Sure they have a lot in common but they perform completely different functions.

Sourcing its water from about a mile away from Loch Nam Bam, Caol Ila is a peaty whisky produced in six tall onion shaped stills and matured in mainly ex-bourbon casks.

Caol Ila has always been an excellent blending whisky and after it was re-built became more of an eyesore than a distillery worth visiting. It is still regarded as the most toasted malt in Scotland and this is difficult to argue against. In recent years there has been an enormous spate of independent bottlings of Caol Ila and for the most part, these bottlings have tended to show Caol Ila to be a lot better than the standard 15 year-old bottling on offer from UDV.

CAOL ILA 15 YEAR-OLD 43%

Nose Toasted peat and malty. Tarmac. Bready.

Palate Sweet peat. Ash and ropey. Medium to heavy body.

Finish Medium finish with an almost unpleasant aftertaste.

Comment There are excellent expressions of Caol Ila that demonstrate it's characteristics better.

Style G

Region Islay

C aol Ila means "the sound of Islay" and its six stills are positioned in a huge window overlooking the sound and commanding arguably the finest view from Islay.

The toasted malt of the northern half of Islay has suffered at times in the hands of its large owner. As a workhorse distillery only a tiny percentage of its whisky gets bottled as a single malt and were it not for the great stocks in the hands of the independent bottlers it would be very difficult to find. Yet some of the greatest whisky I have ever tasted came from the large distillery looking over the Sound of Islay.

Caol Ila Distillery was built in 1846 by Hector Henderson who also had interests in Littlemill. Hector later built Lochindaal on Islay and Camlachie in Glasgow but his entrepreneurial ways got the better of him and his money dried up forcing him to sell in 1852. The distillery was then briefly owned by the proprietors of the Isle of Jura Distillery before coming under the control of Bulloch and Lade Blenders.

Largely demolished apart from the warehouses, Bulloch and Lade rebuilt the distillery in 1879 making use of the newly patented concrete. It was rebuilt again in 1972 by current owners UDV who turned what was one of the most picturesque distilleries into certainly the ugliest on Islay.

Caol Ila has always been a big distillery, which at times has been its downfall. Like Imperial in Speyside it either makes a lot of whisky or none at all. This has meant long silent seasons and on and off closures. It is however a highly prized malt for blending and is included in blends such as Johnnie Walker and Bells.

Caol Ila is the biggest distillery on Islay and easily the smallest name. Yet it is enjoyed by aficionados throughout the world when they can get their hands on it. Independent bottlers such as Signatory and Cadenhead's have been bottling Caol Ila for years with little competition from UDV. Perhaps it is time for Caol Ila, in the face of such popularity of Islay whiskies, to make, not a comeback, but a grand entrance.

Producer UDV *Founded* 1824

Well recognised as a light unpeated malt, Cardhu uses spring water from the Marrich Hill. The spirit is distilled via two of six stills and matured in ex-bourbon casks only.

The whisky produced by Cardhu distillery has always been highly prized by blenders. When Alfred Barnard visited in 1887 he was told, "that a single gallon of it is sufficient to cover ten gallons of plain spirit, and that it commands a high price in the market." It must be noted however that Barnard was not the most subjective journalist and he believed almost every tale that was spun his way on his journey.

If the distillate were as rich as Barnard's guide would have us believe it has certainly changed over the last century. Cardhu is now a fairly light Speyside malt whisky. It is still the heart of Johnnie Walker, although as one journalist put "the soft heart". This has been the case since 1893 when Cardhu was sold to Johnnie Walker.

CARDHU 12 YEAR-OLD 40%

Nose	Malty, floral. Honey. Slight spiciness. Herbal.
Palate	Grassy, spicy. Traces of honey. Light.
Finish	Medium finish with a delicious honey aftertaste.
Comment	Cardhu is… well it's very agreeable. A very agreeable drink.
Style	A

Region Speyside

There have been a number of distilleries with famous women in their histories. Cardhu was lucky enough to have a Mrs Elizabeth Cummings at the helm for nearly 17 years completely rebuilding the distillery in 1884. The original distillery was built in 1824 after John Cummins, the founder, had been convicted of illicit distilling three times. At that time in history that would have been considered his apprenticeship before going legal and the convictions still hang on the office walls today.

John and his wife Helen were a cunning team. While the local excise officer was visiting, often staying at the Cumming's farm, Helen would alert fellow illicit distillers by flying a red flag outside her house while the excise officer was eating, and probably drinking illicit hooch.

In 1922 Cardhu became the first distillery to have oil-fired stills installed. This revolutionary experiment was abandoned after two years - probably due to the increase in availability of gas. The distillery was rebuilt in 1960 although not entirely as some of the 1884 buildings have survived. It now houses a visitor's centre and is one of the UDV showpieces.

Producer UDV Founded 1967

C lynelish (Cline leash) is another distillery in the UDV stable that demands more attention from an ever-growing appreciative public. Fans of this northern malt can often be split into two; those that preferred the peatier Brora and those that like the mustard taste of the current Clynelish. I personally have no preference but completely feel for the consumer who would like to see more expressions of this delicious malt brought out.

A moderately peated malt using water from the Clynemilton Burn, the spirit is distilled via two of six huge stills then left to mature in either ex-bourbon or ex-sherry casks. Some of the casks are left to mature in the dunnage warehouses of the adjoining but now closed Brora Distillery.

Like Caol Ila, Clynelish is bottled en mass by independent bottlers who must find that both distilleries are easy to get casks of and of sufficient consistent quality for bottling. Unlike Caol Ila though, the standard 14 year-old bottling of Clynelish from UDV is rarely bettered by the independent bottlers. Logic would suggest that when you do something well you should exploit your strengths. Well, who ever said large companies had to be logical?!

CLYNELISH 14 YEAR-OLD 43%

Nose Slightly briny. Sweet tar, rubbery (although not unpleasant). Hint of mustard.

Palate Surprisingly soft. Tarry with again that hint of mustard. Medium bodied.

Finish A long, peppery finish.

Comment The finish is akin to Talisker's and it is not hard to see why so many love Clynelish.

Style G

Region *Highlands*

The original Clynelish Distillery was built in 1819 by the Marquis of Stafford, later the First Duke of Sutherland. The Marquis had married into the Sutherland family and illicit distilling was rife in the area of Sutherland. Thus the Marquis tried to get control of the situation by building Clynelish Distillery. The area of Sutherland was affected badly by the Highland Clearances inflicted by the Earls of Sutherland. In 1819, the year that the distillery was built, the Sutherlands burnt 250 crofts and some 500,000 acres were cleared altogether, making way for cattle.

The first license for Clynelish was given to James Harper of Midlothian in 1825. Harper kept the license until 1834 when it was transferred to Andrew Ross until 1846. The distillery changed hands a number of times being rebuilt in 1912 by then owners the Clynelish Distillery Company. The DCL bought up the remaining shares after John Walker & Sons became joint owners of the distillery. It was eventually transferred to the SMD in 1930 and one year later fell silent.

In 1969, after the new Clynelish Distillery was built the original Distillery was renamed Brora, after the town of Brora. The new distillery was built much larger with six stills instead of the two at Brora. Brora continued to operate, distilling a much heavier and peatier whisky, until 1983 when it was mothballed and closed for good.

BRORA DISTILLERY

Producer Inver House   *Founded* 1894

A n Cnoc (An Kock) is the quietest malt from the Inver House portfolio. Still using the same source for spring water from Knock Hill that inspired the distillery to be built over 100 years ago, the distillery has remained small with a single pair of stills. An unpeated malt which is matured in ex-bourbon and ex-sherry casks. It is not the easiest whisky to source due to most of the produce going into blends.

An CNOC *12* YEAR-OLD *40%*

Nose	Grassy. Faintly peaty and sweet toasted caramel.
Palate	Caramel sweetness. Hint of smoke. Light body.
Finish	A quick sweet finish.
Comment	A smooth unpretentious dram.
Style	**B**

An Cnoc is the Gaelic spelling of Knockdhu, which means 'Black Hill'. The distillery was built at the peak of the whisky boom in 1894 to supply whisky to the Haig Blending Company (who were later owned by UDV). It is the only distillery built by DCL as all of the others were acquired in the depression periods of the early 20th Century.

At the time the DCL was all about grain distilling and needed to secure enough malt whisky for the major blends of the day. The owner of the Knock estate had discovered a rather decent spring well and after having the water analysed DCL got involved and like Auchroisk (built some 80 years later) a distillery was built due to the excellent water source.

Knockdhu stayed in the control of UDV until closing in 1983 and then being bought by Inver House and reopened in 1989. Under the new owners the single malt has been able to flourish, albeit in a small and discreet manner. The water is from the same spring that the farmer found over a century ago and the local village of Knock receives the same water through their taps.

During the last war Knockdhu was used to house servicemen. For almost the duration of the war the distillery played host to a unit from the Indian Army. They no doubt enjoyed the Scottish climate but were given special privileges such as setting up their own slaughterhouse to prepare halal meat in accordance with their religion.

Producer UDV *Founded* 1869

Cragganmore has always been an enigmatic whisky, an almost chameleon dram with so many side attractions that one could get lost in all its wiles. This subtleness has to be partly due to the relatively hard water from the Craggan Burn, and the four unusually shaped flat topped stills and strange lyne arms that are T-shaped and not sloped, resulting in a lighter, dryer spirit. The distillery, like Dalwhinnie and Talisker, also uses external worm tubs allowing extra contact with copper before being put into the cask.

Whatever the reasons are for Cragganmore's unique style are probably best left unknown. Don't want to slay the proverbial golden goose and as history has shown what works for one distillery may not always work for others.

CRAGGANMORE *12 YEAR-OLD 43%*

The Speyside representative of the Six Classics.

Nose	Soft, buttery. Floral, creamy and a hint of smoke. Sugary.
Palate	Sweet, spicy, fruity. Spiky. Medium bodied.
Finish	Short finish, but sweet and chewy.
Comment	This dram changes each time I try it. Sometimes smoky sometimes sweet, always delicious.
Style	C

CRAGGANMORE *1984 DISTILLER'S EDITION 40%*

Finished in Port pipes.

Nose	Soft, smoky heather and honey. Minty oak notes. Nettles.
Palate	Licorice. Bready. Soft and medium bodied.
Finish	Short, clean finish.
Comment	The Port pipes have added that minty flavour. Still complex but I prefer the 12 year-old.
Style	E

Region Speyside

The founder of Cragganmore was a giant of a man. Weighing in at a staggering 22 stone (308lb's), Smith had to ride in the guard's van on the train, as he was too large for the passenger section. He also had a special leather armchair built to accommodate his freakish frame. Rumour has it that the large stone at the entrance to Cragganmore Distillery was put there by Smith who had uncovered it while ploughing a field.

Smith built the first Cragganmore Distillery in 1869 after the owner of the estate and Ballindalloch Castle granted him the rights. The owners of the castle could often be seen replacing their cask of maturing Cragganmore when and if they needed. An old smuggling bothy was incorporated into the distillery as the spirit-receiving room. Smith also made good use of the railway explosion. Cragganmore was the first distillery to have its own private siding right up to the distillery.

John Smith died in 1887 and his son Gordon Smith took over the role of distillery manager. In 1901 the distillery was rebuilt with the help of Charles Doig, an expert on the design and improvements of distilleries. Despite the help of the inventor and architect the distillery remained fairly untouched by modern improvements. Indeed despite electricity being installed in 1919 the distillery was still ordering parts for their waterwheel and steam engine as late as 1950.

Cragganmore came under the ownership of the Distillers Company Ltd in 1927 via its link with White Horse Distillers. Eventually this led to being part of United Distillers and Vintners (UDV) and being chosen as the Speyside representative for the Six Classics. It had very stiff competition for this role and, had Mortlach in Dufftown been a more picturesque distillery it may have won the title and enjoyed greater exposure.

Producer *Kyndal Spirits* **Founded** *1839*

Over the last ten years Dalmore Single Highland Malt has been strongly associated with sherry wood and this is reflected in many of their different expressions, namely the 12 year-old Cigar Malt and the 30 year-old. The Dalmore 12 year-old allocates 30% specially selected oloroso sherry butts from Gonzalez Byass, Spain and this increases to 60% in their Dalmore Cigar Malt; the remaining ratios are made up from American White oak.

The question of whisky and cigars has raged long and hard with non-smokers in one corner and cigar advocates such as Whisky Magazine in the other. I have tried my hardest to pair whiskies and cigars but I can't - it is better left up to those consumers who can take the heavy cigar smoke, although I have been advised Montecristo, Upmann and Romeo y Julieta are the most compatible.

DALMORE 12 YEAR-OLD 43%

Nose	Cherries. Fruitcake. Marmalade and Marzipan. Thick malt extract.
Palate	Salty-sweet, oily and rich. Bitter fruitcake taste with a sensual orange finish. Quite heavy.
Finish	Bittersweet lemony honey aftertaste.
Comment	Quite a developed 12 year-old baring little similarity to any of its neighbours.
Style	F

DALMORE CIGAR MALT 43%

Nose	Rich stewed fruits. Caramel. Malty and oaky. Sherry comes sauntering through tardy to the party!
Palate	Malt loaf, fruitcake. Heavy and citrus. Quite rich.
Finish	Long finish, tingly and warming. A licorice aftertaste that simply won't go away!
Comment	A great whisky that seems most suitable to be enjoyed with a cigar. Has so much depth that it is difficult to follow. Not that I am complaining!
Style	F

Region *Highlands*

The coastal distillery of Dalmore was built in 1839 by Alexander Matheson on land that had previously been farmed. The distillery is thought to have been operated by a Mrs Margaret Sutherland in its earliest days before the Mackenzie Bros bought it in 1878. The stag's head logo that adorns the bottles of Dalmore whisky is taken from the Mackenzie's coat of arms . Legend has it that the chief of the Mackenzie clan saved King Alexander III from a charging stag while hunting.

The Mackenzies were thought to have been friendly with James Whyte and Charles Mackay and the companies were merged in 1960 to form the Dalmore-Whyte & Mackay which eventually became Whyte & Mackay Distillers. The distillery was commandeered in WW1 and used by the Admiralty on behalf of the US Navy as a base for the manufacture of deep-sea mines. Towards the end of the war part of the distillery was damaged in an explosion. The repairs took four years to complete and Dalmore did not return to productivity until 1922.

Dalmore had its own Saladin box maltings installed in 1956 that eventually closed in 1981 sourcing all of the malt commercially. Dalmore is thought to mean 'big meadowland' having taken parts from Norse and Gaelic. Water is taken from the River Alness which has been the source since 1839. Anyone wishing to tour a distillery should bear Dalmore in mind as summed up by Duncan & Wendy Graham in their book "Visiting Distilleries":

"They come no better than this. Prepare to devote time and enjoy the perfect tour. A feast for your eye and nose."

Producer UDV *Founded* 1897

O n a recent trip to Dalwhinnie the whisky was described as 'grandma's malt'. A fair summation of a delightful, soft, mouth full of sweet, grassy notes that always leaves a pleasant taste in the mouth. Using water from a loch spring, Alt an t'Sluie, this is a lightly peated whisky produced via two broad onion shaped stills and outdoor condensers.

In recent times UDV has offered the idea of serving Dalwhinnie chilled. This has caused a split of opinion right down the middle. While I think it has frozen out all of the flavour and left all of the bitterness others have enjoyed the smoothness that the chilling brings.

DALWHINNIE 15 YEAR-OLD 43%

The Highlands representative for the Six Classic's.

Nose	Light, spirity and very grassy. Green and heathery.
Palate	Sweet at first - Heathery and light.
Finish	Quite an oaky, warming finish.
Comment	Despite being aged for a minimum of 15 years this expression has a very young, fresh nose. A nice, light whisky.
Style	A

DALWHINNIE 1980 DISTILLER'S EDITION 43%

Finished in Oloroso casks.

Nose	Chewy malt. Hint of mint. Heathery. Dry sherry notes.
Palate	Soft, buttery. Bittersweet. Light body.
Finish	Short, grassy finish.
Comment	Definitely Dalwhinnie - this expression is worth the extra treatment it receives.
Style	C

Region Highlands

Tasted blind most of us would be guessing that Dalwhinnie was distilled a few miles south of its location off the A9 in central Scotland. With it's sweet, floral and grassy notes the whisky belies its position as the highest distillery in Scotland. Yet Dalwhinnie stands triumphantly against the bare scenery between the Monadhlaith, Cairngorm and Grampian Mountains. At 326m (1,073ft) above sea level, marketers would have us believe that it is the drastic seasonal temperature changes that create the unusual softness in this highland dram. I'd beg to argue that it has more to do with the soft water and still shape and maybe the outdoor worm tubs.

Dalwhinnie is thought to mean 'meeting place' probably due to the village of the same name being the crossroads of several roads previously used by everything from smugglers to shepherds. It would be safe to say that the area, pre-legal distilling, was swarming with illicit distillers.

Dalwhinnie began production in 1897 and was originally called Strathspey despite the distillery being 25 miles from Speyside. The River Spey however passes just a few feet away from the distillery after rising in the Monadhlaith Mountains to the west. Dalwhinnie's first incarnation was not overly successful and eventually sold out to Cook & Bernheimer in 1905. At the time the US firm were the largest distillers across the pond. Unfortunately for the firm, prohibition was only a decade and a half away and signalled the end of the US interest in Dalwhinnie.

After changing hands more times than a rugby ball, Dalwhinnie finally succumbed to the whirlpool suction of the DCL and began a steady career in the production of whisky. After being chosen to be the Highland representative in the Six Classics it received the royal treatment in the form of a new visitors centre in 1992. It would be unfair to say that Dalwhinnie was anything short of one of the best distilleries to visit. Just be mindful of the winter months - the snow can get very deep!

Producer Burn Stewart Distillers **Founded** 1965

Deanston is an unpeated malt, although some traces of peat can be found via its water source the River Teith. The river is further utilised by driving two turbines to supply all their electricity, any surplus power goes to the National Grid. Deanston operates an open top mash tun on a long cycle that yields dark sweet wort. The spirit then passes through two of the four large bulbous stills then is left to mature in either ex-bourbon or ex-sherry casks

Deanston has had little 'airplay' and is not the easiest whisky to find. This is largely due to a shortage of stock and the high demand for it from blenders. Deanston is an excellent individual dram with some unique tastes, and now that more stock is available, it should become easier to find.

And what is even better for the consumer is that by far the best expression is the younger (and therefore cheaper) 12 year-old. Not all good things come to those who wait after all! As Burn Stewart fight their way out of a corner and recover to push their brands don't be surprised to hear the name Deanston mentioned a bit more in future.

DEANSTON 12 YEAR-OLD 40%

Nose   A hint of smoke over fruits of the forest. Fresh and minty. Liqueur-ish.

Palate   Does not disappoint on the palate. Brief reminder of smoke followed by berries.

Finish   A minty, spicy finish that lingers just long enough to keep the mind intrigued.

Comment   Quite superb. Pleases all over and throughout. I could definitely get used to this!

Style   C

DEANSTON 17 YEAR-OLD 40%

Nose   Cereal notes. Vanilla and banana chips. Traces of oak. Creamy.

Palate   Creamy at first then a hint of banana. Medium bodied.

Finish   Long finish that tingles and warms with a creamy aftertaste.

Comment   Remarkably different from the 12 year-old which I prefer considerably.

Style   B

Region Highlands

Deanston Distillery was built, or rather converted, in the middle of the 1960's in the first boom period the whisky industry experienced since the turn of the century. Richard Arkwright, the inventor of the spinning frame, designed the buildings that house the distillery. The distillery was converted from the Arkwright cotton mill by the Deanston Distillery Co Ltd a subsidiary of James Finlay.

Finlay retained ownership until 1972 when it was sold to Invergordon Distillers. Invergordon managed to keep the stills firing for ten years before the distillery went silent from 1982 - 1990 when the current owners, Burn Stewart Distillers bought it and put it back to work.

Deanston Distillery is quite remarkable to look at and even more remarkable inside. One of the warehouses used to be a vaulted weaving shed built in 1836. Its walls are more than one meter thick causing the temperature inside the building to stay fairly constant all year-round. In converting the mill to a distillery four floors had to be removed to accommodate the stills and machinery.

Being situated in Doune, Deanston Distillery will always find it hard to become a tourist attraction. Doune Castle lies nearby and having been the location of films such as Monty Python and the Holy Grail tourists will often overlook the strange distillery that few people have ever heard of.

Producer *Speyside Distillery Company* **Founded** *1991*

Drumguish (Drum oo ish) is the younger representative from the Speyside Distillery. It is one of the maltiest drams around and lovers of fresh, full-flavoured whiskies will find they will prefer Drumguish to the new Speyside 10 year-old. If everyone agrees with my notes we may see a mixed reaction from Speyside Distillery.

On the one hand they will want a 10 year-old whisky to compete in the biggest sector of the single malt market. However, if they can secure enough sales with the younger expression of their whisky then the monetary returns to the company will be far greater. Perhaps, however, Drumguish will now die a death as Speyside 10 year-old takes its place. This would be a shame.

DRUMGUISH 40%

This whisky is 3 to 5 years old.

Nose	Heaps of malt and honey. Malt extract. Barley.
Palate	Does not follow through on the palate what is promised on the nose. Still a lovely malty taste however.
Finish	Long. New-make finish.
Comment	Very drinkable for five years. The malty flavours stick to the mouth.
Style	C

Region *Highlands*

Speyside is the second youngest distillery in Scotland and is a dream-come-true for George Christie. Christie started to fulfil his dream back in 1955 when he formed the Speyside Distillery & Bonding Co. A year later the distillery site was acquired near Kingussie at Drumguish, the name given to the first malt whisky bottled by the company. The building of the distillery began in 1962; an extension was built in 1980 but it wasn't until 1987 that the distillery was completed.

It took another three years before the first spirit ran from the two pot stills on December 12 1990. The distillery had taken the best part of four decades to complete and finally now in 2002 the company has what it desperately wanted; it's own 10 year-old single malt whisky. Anyone thinking of building their own distillery should sit up and take notice.

The current Speyside Distillery is named after a previous Speyside Distillery that was also situated in Kingussie. The former distillery was built in 1895 although it only survived until 1911 when it was subsequently dismantled and demolished. The current distillery sits near the A9 that runs through the middle of central Scotland which means despite its name the whisky is not a Speyside whisky.

Producer *Signatory Vintage Scotch Whisky Co. Ltd* **Founded** *1837*

The only trace of peat in Edradour comes from the spring water of nearby Moulin Moor. The malt is unpeated and the spirit is distilled via a single pair of the smallest stills possible. A purifier is used to lighten the spirit before setting it into ex-sherry casks to mature.

As with Dalmore, I am convinced that Edradour (rhymes with hour) has transformed over the last few years into a completely different whisky. Some tasting notes I dug out from a couple years ago back me up; 'Slightly sweet, hint of sherry. Honey. White wine notes.' They could be from different distilleries. The cask policy must have changed somewhere down the line for Edradour and we are now seeing a large proportion of sherry butts in the mix.

All of this has meant that Edradour can now compete against The Macallan and Glendronach for the title of the richest whisky. Edradour is very drinkable despite the powerful sherry nose. From the smallest legal distillery in Scotland comes one of the most drinkable whiskies.

EDRADOUR 10 YEAR-OLD 40%

Nose	Powerful rich sherry, vanilla and tangerine smells. Cake icing. Extremely sweet.
Palate	Soft icing. Sumptuous vanilla. Quite dry and heavy.
Finish	Medium finish with a delicious soft vanilla aftertaste.
Comment	This is a whisky that should spend more time in the mouth than being sniffed. Utterly delicious - savour it, but definitely drink it!
Style	F

Region *Highlands*

Scotland's smallest distillery is also one of the most visited. The distillery only produces in one year what a large distillery can produce in one week. Remembering that every visitor receives a free dram at the end of the tour, there must be quite a large percentage of Edradour's whisky that goes to the one hundred thousand visitors that trek through the small distillery each year!

This does mean that although it is a picturesque distillery tours are often squashed and cramped - don't let that stop you going though. It is fascinating to see the entire process as it would have appeared to the farmers of old (although the whisky is a mite better now than it would have been!).

Edradour claims to have been founded in 1825 although the distillery dates later than that. The distillery has always remained small with just two stills. The distillery is so small that it only takes three employees to run it (one of them being the manager). Everything is done by hand including the shovelling of the draff into the farmers trailer; possibly a sight you will not see at a distillery anywhere else in the world.

The distillery has the oldest working Morton refrigerator in the world, although that only appeals to people who like such things. For the rest of us, 1982 was the key date in the distillery's history as Edradour was bought by Pernod Ricard and became part of the portfolio of Chivas Brothers. In 2002 the distillery again changed hands and is now owned by A. Symington of Signatory Vintage Scotch Whisky Co. Ltd.

Producer *Allied Distillers* **Founded** *1826*

Glendronach is one of only a few distilleries on the mainland that still uses traditional malting floors, producing 12% of its own malt that is lightly peated. Water from the Dronac Burn is used for mashing then the spirit is distilled via two pairs of swan necked stills. Only ex-sherry casks are used for maturation.

Glendronach is also only one of a few distilleries which matures its malt entirely in ex-sherry casks. While I find the sherry flavours too much, others will want nothing less. "Vive la difference" as they say. If you are looking for anything more, let the whisky breathe a bit and you should detect a hint of phenols coming through with a very pleasant and lingering aftertaste.

This is a very affordable and drinkable 15 year-old single malt, which does well in the markets that like sherried whiskies such as Germany and America. The sherried richness also proves popular with many who are being introduced to single malt whisky for the first time.

GLENDRONACH 15 YEAR-OLD 40%

Matured entirely in ex-sherry casks.

Nose	Stewed fruits, raisins. Sherry and caramel. Nutty notes & vanilla. Background notes of citrus.
Palate	Sherry surges past all of the other flavours. Heavy though not overly oily.
Finish	Orange liqueur finish.
Comment	An intriguing malt. Let the whisky breath and watch it come to life.
Style	F

Region *Highlands*

The distillery takes its name from the Dronac Burn whose banks it lies upon. The distillery changed hands a number of times after being licensed to James Allardes in 1826 until being sold to the fifth son of William Grant of Glenfiddich fame. Glendronach stayed in the Grant's control until 1960 when William Teachers & sons acquired it. Teacher's was later acquired by Allied in 1976. Allied have managed to preserve many of the traditional methods at Glendronach including malting floors, wooden washbacks, coal-fired stills and earthen floored dunage warehouses, making it a picturesque distillery to visit.

Allied have made considerable investment into the industry including making their Miltonduff Distillery the most technologically advanced malt distillery and making their bottling operation at Dumbarton the first fully integrated site in the Scotch whisky industry.

Although Glendronach has been mothballed for some time, it is due to restart production later this year (2002) this will help ensure stocks remain high of this great whisky

Producer J & G *Grant* **Founded** 1836

Glenfarclas has long enjoyed its niche markets throughout the world and over time this has forged a reputation of excellence for Glenfarclas whisky. Glenfarclas is a relatively small distiller and is often overlooked while the Macallans and Glenmorangies of this world sweep up the large market shares. This will change in time however, as the whisky of this distillery is too good and readily available worldwide.

Produced from lightly peated malt, steeped in Saladin box maltings and using slightly peated spring water from the Green Burn on Ben Rinnes. Glenfarclas has six of the largest direct fired pot stills on Speyside and uses outdoor condensers. The final malt is a spirit which has matured in ex-sherry and ex-bourbon casks.

Being an independent company has its advantages for Glenfarclas who are able to chop and change their bottling strategy when and if they like. Considering none of the whiskies listed below are 'finishes' it is surprising to see how many different ages Glenfarclas bottle (and there are a few more than that). This allows the consumer to determine the premium age for Glenfarclas. For me the 10 year-old is one of the best, although the 30 year-old does demonstrate that whisky can grow old gracefully. Why not try them all and decide for yourself?

GLENFARCLAS **105 60%**

This whisky is around 8 years old.

Nose	Vanilla fudge and raisins. Trifle.
Palate	Custard creaminess. Sherry. Full bodied and flavoured.
Finish	Long sweet finish (again reminding me of trifle).
Comment	At 60% it is surprisingly palatable. A very close relative to the 10 year-old.
Style	D

GLENFARCLAS **10** *YEAR-OLD* **40%**

Nose	Delicious malt and sherry notes. Fruitcake. Vanilla fudge and raisins.
Palate	Medium to full bodied. Pleasantly bitter.
Finish	Medium finish with a long licorice aftertaste.
Comment	One of the finest 10 year-old expressions on Speyside!
Style	D

Region Speyside

GLENFARCLAS 15 YEAR-OLD 46%

Nose	Malty. Earthy. Dried apricots. Spiky. Sherry.
Palate	Spiky, tingly - quite light. A little sharp and firm.
Finish	Gentle finish with an oily aftertaste.
Comment	Similar to Longmorn on the nose. A charming dram

Style   B

GLENFARCLAS 21 YEAR-OLD 43%

Nose	Brandy butter and trifle. Floral notes with undertones of sweet oak and coconut.
Palate	Velvet oakiness and sweet dried fruit. Medium bodied. Very smooth.
Finish	Medium finish with red wine flavours. Quite dry.
Comment	This expression is quite subtle for a 21 year-old. It tastes as if some remarkable casks were vatted in this bottling.

Style   D

GLENFARCLAS 25 YEAR-OLD 43%

Nose	Battenburg cake. Marzipan, vanilla. Spirity. Icing sugar.
Palate	Spiky. Chewy oak. Medium bodied and mouth coating.
Finish	Quick finish but with a licorice root aftertaste.
Comment	Not as graceful as the 21 year-old or as punchy as the 30 year-old but stands alone with it's cake-like tastes.

Style   D

GLENFARCLAS 30 YEAR-OLD 43%

Nose	Rich honey and mulled wine spices. Toffee and caramel. A rich sugary sweetness.
Palate	Everything promised on the nose is delivered on the palate. All the toffee and honey and spices! Tingly and warming.
Finish	Medium finish but sweet throughout. Sweet licorice aftertaste.
Comment	The oldest whisky tasted in the book demonstrates why we will pay more for age. A very rewarding dram.

Style   F

Region Speyside

Glenfarclas, meaning the 'Valley of the Green Land', is the second oldest family owned distillery in Scotland. Sitting in the Rechlerich Farm on the Ballindalloch Estate the distillery lies on the flanks of Ben Rinnes where Glenfarclas takes its water. The original distillery was built on the farm by Robert Hay in 1836 and was subsequently purchased for £511.19s by John Grant (no relation to the other Grant distilling dynasties) in 1865. The farm was an ideal staging post for drovers from the Glenlivet area on their way to Elgin who could water their cattle and quench their own thirst with a dram of Glenfarclas 105 cask strength.

Toward the turn of the 20th Century John Grant's two sons expanded the distillery from originally distilling 50,000 gallons per year to an annual capacity of around 300,000 gallons. This was around the time of the great whisky boom. Despite having entered into an agreement with the ill-fated Pattison's, they managed to weather the depression and Pattison crash of 1898.

Further expansions took place in 1960 and again 1972 resulting in Glenfarclas now being one of the largest distilleries in Scotland, operating the largest stills on Speyside and possibly the largest mash tun in the industry. The distilleries draff pipes are so large that in order to clean them the distillery fires footballs down them!

Today the distillery is owned by the fifth generation of Grant's, John L S Grant and is still registered to J & G Grant. Each generation has called their sons either John or George; hence the company has always rightfully kept its name. Due to its independence, the company is able to change its strategies rapidly and keep up with consumer demand. Glenfarclas were one of the first distilleries to open their doors to visitors and now sport a luxurious visitor centre complete with a pagoda head from their old kiln and a dining room that is furnished using oak panelling from the Canadian Pacific liner "Empress of Australia".

Producer *William Grant & Sons* **Founded** *1887*

Glenfiddich is one of the most recognisable drams from Scotland. Whenever it comes up in a blind tasting competition it is a sigh of relief to the entrants. The nose on the 12 year-old is similar to all of the other expressions and it is testament to the entire team at Glenfiddich for their consistency and excellence.

Lightly peated with water from the Robbie Due spring, Glenfiddich operate 28 stills in trios, with their spirit stills being so small they need two spirit stills to every wash still. A combination of ex-bourbon and ex-sherry casks are used along with new oak, from which the various expressions are married.

Glenfiddich often gets rubbished by newly appointed single malt connoisseurs and even the best of us at times have tended to sneer at the mass-produced whisky. This is all in error however as Glenfiddich is not the best selling single malt in the world just because it's marketing is good. The dram is always good and often exceptional. When Glenfiddich gets older it develops a fruity dimension to its character that is par excellence. Don't sneer at it, pour it and drink it and enjoy it!

GLENFIDDICH 12 YEAR-OLD SPECIAL RESERVE 40%

Nose	Unmistakable Glenfiddich character of sweet heather-honey with a fresh slightly green aroma and background spices.
Palate	Waves of honey with a hint of spice in each wave.
Finish	A short and slightly bitter finish - but not overly unpleasant.
Comment	A very accomplished and stylish dram that deserves to be No.1.
Style	C

Region *Speyside*

GLENFIDDICH 15 YEAR-OLD SOLERA RESERVE 40%

Made with whisky from largely ex-sherry casks and a small number of ex-bourbon casks that are vatted in new oak for four months before being vatted further in a large Solera vat.

Nose	Bucket loads of honey with a suggestion of sherry. Pleasant and herbal.
Palate	Shades of new wood overpowering the sherry.
Finish	The sherry returns in a triumphant finish that is sweet and lingers deliciously.
Comment	Too sweet for some palates but a completely different whisky to any other Glenfiddich expressions.
Style	F

GLENFIDDICH 18 YEAR-OLD ANCIENT RESERVE 43%

Nose	Mulled wine spices with sweet oak and surprise, surprise… honey.
Palate	Very sweet and oaky.
Finish	A fruity, citrusy, finish that lingers warmingly.
Comment	The fruit that is prevalent in older Glenfiddichs rears it's aromatic head in this expression. For anyone who doubts Glenfiddich's pedigree this is a dram to savour and re-evaluate.
Style	C

Region Speyside

Glenfiddich has been the biggest selling single malt whisky for more than 30 years and eases around 750,000 cases of whisky out of its on-site bottling plant each year. Glenfiddich is a giant of a drink and all of us that enjoy single malt whisky should pay homage.

Glenfiddich's dalliance with malt whisky began in 1963 when William Grant & Sons made the bold step of marketing their single malt whisky. Now it is enjoyed in more than 200 countries around the globe and their initial bravery has paved the way for others to join suit.

It is hard to imagine that this great company was started by one man who, after serving his apprenticeship at Mortlach Distillery saved enough money to build Glenfiddich (meaning 'Valley of the deer'). From such humble beginnings William Grant & Sons now own five distilleries (Glenfiddich, Balvenie, Convalmore, Girvan and Kininivie which is the most recently built in 1992) operating four of them; one of them being the largest grain distillery in Europe based at Girvan.

Glenfiddich operate their stills in trios: one wash still and two differently shaped stills for its spirit stills; a reflux ball still and a gas mantle still. This tradition dates back to 1887 when Cardhu were refitting their distillery and sold off all of their old equipment to William Grant - the purchase included the odd number of stills.

The 28 stills (the most in any malt distillery in the world) are split into two rooms with traditional coal-fired stills in Still House 1 and gas-fired stills in Still House 2. After experimentation to see whether or not the labour intensive coal-firing method actually imparts a different flavour on the wash and spirit, it was concluded there was no difference.

Every aspect of the distilling process is carried out on site (if you include the floor maltings at Balvenie). There is a cooperage and a bottling plant (Springbank is the only other Scottish distillery to bottle on site) that bottles all of the Glenfiddich and some of the small batch bottlings.

Producer *Morrison Bowmore Distillers* **Founded** *1797*

I t is very rare that I, or anyone, discover a whisky that promises so much on the nose that to drink it would almost be a sin. One such Glen Garioch (Glen Geary) does that for me. A bottling by the Scotch Malt Whisky Society of an October 1979 distillation then aged after 17 years in a port pipe until the whisky was 19 years old and then bottled at a cask strength of 46.8%.

Chances are you won't get to try this whisky but you can try all of the proprietary bottlings of Glen Garioch. The 10, 15 and 21 expressions all have similar Glen Garioch characteristics; a medium to heavy and oily body with delicious sweet peat and fruits of the forest in a fresh mint sauce.

This is a malt whisky of the true Highland style. Using water from the Parcock Hills the whisky is made in two large lantern shaped stills and two spirit still incorporating a boil ball to help produce a lighter spirit. The malt is then matured in ex-bourbon casks. It is a whisky that is such an uncovered treasure that I am reluctant to share it. Go buy it though; lots of it, and then the distillery will be forced to continue in full production. Perhaps then they can finish a few casks in a port pipe and you can all discover what the whisky I have referred to tastes like!

GLEN GARIOCH 10 YEAR-OLD 40%

Nose	Cloves, spirity. Minty. Earthy and leafy.
Palate	Sweet, medium bodied. Nutty.
Finish	Bittersweet finish with a hint of cloves.
Comment	All the smell of Autumn and a delightful palate to match. Not as fulfilled as the 15 year-old however.
Style	E

Region *Highlands*

GLEN GARIOCH 15 YEAR-OLD 43%

Nose   Minty & herbal. Spices, icing sugar. Fruits of the forest. Wild berries.

Palate   Icing sugar. Minty. Medium to heavy body.
Utterly delicious when allowed to warm a little.

Finish   Long, fruity, sugary finish. Makes you want more.

Comment   A stunning whisky that offers so much individuality. Fantastic.

Style   E

GLEN GARIOCH 21 YEAR-OLD 43%

Nose   Icing sugar. Minty. Fennel.

Palate   Mint with aniseed. Medium bodied. Tongue tingly.

Finish   Aniseed. Medium, sweeties finish.

Comment   The extra six years haven't done much more. Still superb however.

Style   E

Region *Highlands*

The distillery dates back to 1797 and has had an unremarkable history. It was once owned by Sanderson of Vat 69 fame and then moved into the hands of the DCL who sold it to Stanley Morrison due to water shortage. Morrison swiftly dug a new well and increased output threefold showing the shortcoming in DCL's policy.

Glen Garioch has suffered under the might of its sister brands in the Morrison Bowmore portfolio (Bowmore and Auchentoshan being the others). It even stopped production for a couple years. Thankfully however it is now working like a Trojan once again and the might of Glen Garioch whisky shall long continue.

The distillery was once famed for growing some of the greatest batches of tomatoes in Scotland. It achieved this by building huge greenhouses adjacent to the distillery and warming it with waste heat from the distillery. It also used the excess Carbon Dioxide to feed the growing tomatoes. At one point the distillery was producing around 180 tons of tomatoes a year. This was obviously no little hobby of the distillery managers.

Situated just outside Aberdeen in a town called Oldmeldrum, Glen Garioch is now using a lower peating level for the whisky than before. This may see the end of a great tradition of using a heavily peated malt, that has set Glen Garioch apart from surrounding distilleries. At least though it is back to full production again.

Producer *The Edrington Group* **Founded** *1833*

Well marketed as an unpeated malt made with water from Loch Carron, the spirit passes through two of three stills and is matured in ex-sherry and refill whisky casks.

It isn't often that both sides of a coin can maintain marketability. The whisky industry does present marketers with such a challenge. At the moment it is extremely fashionable to like and drink the heavily peated and dark whiskies (just look at the cult status of whiskies like Laphroaig and Bowmore Black). Almost in the same breath however, PR and marketing companies are stressing that their whiskies are light in colour and completely non-peated.

I cannot think of another industry that has a similar situation. Glengoyne enjoys its PR as a light and completely non-peated whisky. Strangely the distillery could call itself a Highland or a Lowland whisky as the whisky is made just north of the Highland Line and is matured in the Lowlands. The distillery also used to be triple distilled changing, perhaps to be more like a Highland malt.

Despite Glengoyne's PR managers insisting that the whisky is completely smoke-free, many drinkers equally insist that they detect a smokiness in Glengoyne. I am on the side of the marketers, as I do not detect a smoky quality to Glengoyne. Either way Glengoyne is a pretty fine whisky regardless.

GLENGOYNE *10* YEAR-OLD *40%*

Nose	Spices. Heather. Brandy notes. Soft. Coconut. Apples.
Palate	Soft and sweet. Not overly oily or complex. Nutty. Light - medium body.
Finish	A long, bittersweet finish.
Comment	A nice dram that will suit most palates.
Style	C

Region *Highlands*

GLENGOYNE 17 YEAR-OLD 43%

Nose	Oranges and lemons. Briny. Sherry, toffee, apricots, sugared almonds.
Palate	Sweet oak, apricots. Stewed fruits. Medium bodied.
Finish	Long finish with just a hint of oakiness towards the end.
Comment	Better than the 10 year-old. Even by being non-peated the whisky is still not light. Quite superb.
Style	**D**

GLENGOYNE 21 YEAR-OLD 43%

Nose	Peach skin, apricot. Oak & spice. Bubble gum.
Palate	Spices, oak (bitter). Light-medium body.
Finish	Gentle finish.
Comment	Not an improvement on the 17 year-old which only goes to show how good the 17 year-old is.
Style	**D**

Region Highlands

The distillery was originally called Glenguin when it was licensed in 1833. The area was a prime target for illicit distillers although there must have been heavy attention from the excise officers due to the close proximity of Glasgow. When the Lang Bros bought the distillery in 1876 the distillery was called Burnfoot. Lang reverted back to the original name and then in 1905 changed the name to Glengoyne.

Glengoyne is similar to Macallan in its use of small low wines stills and also in using Golden Promise barley. Whether or not there can be any similarities between the Glengoyne and Macallan spirits is probably best left to scientific speculation (none exist for me).

Glengoyne has perhaps one of the oddest set-ups of any of the distilleries in Scotland. It is owned and operated by the Lang Bros who are in turn a subsidiary of Robertson & Baxter whose parent company is The Edrington Group. If that wasn't confusing enough the company that looks after the distribution and to some extent the PR and marketing of Glengoyne is Berry Bros & Rudd. And it is probably more confusing than that!

At the end of the tour (which is one of the best) drams can be taken looking over the 50ft waterfall into the pool behind the distillery. Water from the falls was originally used for distillation, but is now only used for cooling. The distillery is one of the most picturesque distilleries in Scotland and due to its location near to Loch Lomond and Glasgow it is also one of the most visited. The distillery is possibly unique, by having its own helipad. With Glengoyne being so close to Glasgow this has to be for the laziest of visitors!

Producer *Chivas Brothers* **Founded** *1840*

A lightly peated malt, made with spring water from the Caperdonich Springs. Glen Grant operates four mushroom shaped and four onion shaped stills incorporating boil balls and purifiers. The resulting spirit is very light.

Glen Grant enjoys success in markets that enjoy their whisky young and light. Countries such as Italy, Spain and to some extent France, like their whisky in a tall glass mixed with something cold and sweet as a brief respite from the hot Mediterranean sun. Thus Glen Grant get returns on their stock in five years. Compared to others who have to wait at least 10-15 years to see a return on their stock.

The non-aged expression is predominantly aged in ex-bourbon casks and this is evident most noticeably in the lack of colour in the whisky. The 10 year-old has a larger number of sherry casks used in the vatting but this is not overly evident in the whisky. This is not a complaint rather I commend Glen Grant for producing a very fragrant and appetizing whisky. This one won't go with steak or a cigar but suits the role of aperitif or lunchtime malt with charm and dignity.

GLEN GRANT 40%

This expression is around 5 years old.

Nose	Licorice root, nettles. A fresh, green aroma with gentle spices.
Palate	Quite oily. Very young and fresh. Light body.
Finish	A soft, elegant finish.
Comment	A taste of the garden.
Style	A

GLEN GRANT 10 YEAR-OLD 40%

Nose	Hint of smoke, grassy. Earthy. Aniseed, boiled sweets.
Palate	Creamy, bitter but pleasant. Light in body.
Finish	Medium finish with aniseed aftertaste.
Comment	A natural progression from the younger expression. A nice, individual malt whisky.
Style	A

Region *Speyside*

The distillery was built by John & James Grant in 1840 having been in partnership with John & James Walker at Aberlour Distillery. The distillery quickly became renowned for its superior whisky and the Grant's decision to build big paid off. After the death of John (1864) and then James (1872) the distillery passed on to James Grant Jr., otherwise known as Major Grant. Major Grant had collected flowers and plants on his travels in India and Africa and, on returning, constructed a garden on the premises of the distillery. The garden was restored in 1995 and is now open to the public. The Major outlived his entire family and the distillery went to his grandson Douglas Mackessack. Mackessack retired on January 31, 1978 when Seagram's bought out the distillery, thus ending the 138-year run for the Grant family.

Over the years Glen Grant has been continually expanded. It is now capable of producing 2 million gallons a year and for a while had the unique responsibility of having a second distillery with the same name. Glen Grant No 2, as it was imaginatively called, was built in 1897 by the Grants literally across the road. The whisky, under the insistence of the Excise, was pumped across in a pipeline (only during the daylight hours) from Glen Grant No 2 to Glen Grant. Later, due to the Pattison Crash and the drop in demand for whisky, Glen Grant No 2 was mothballed. That was until 1965 when it was reopened and renamed Caperdonich after the well that had originally fed the Glen Grant Distillery.

Glen Grant has a 5 year-old whisky which has been enjoying success in Italy for a long time. Indeed Glen Grant was one of the first distilleries to bottle a single malt whisky before the boom in the 80's. Glen Grant, and Caperdonich, are both now owned by Chivas Brothers. The signs for Glen Grant are good, as it will only complement Chivas Brothers current portfolio of whiskies. It will almost be like having a Lowland whisky to market.

Producer *Chivas Brothers* **Founded** *1957*

G len Keith has only ever had two expressions bottled by previous owners Seagram's. The first was a whisky distilled pre 1983, which is now very hard to find. The later expression is the 10 year-old bottled at 43%. This is an uncomplicated whisky that slides down the throat with consummate ease. It is no wonder that it was a good blending whisky but also as a single malt it is a very pleasing whisky.

Using an unpeated malt, the spirit is made with water from the Newmill spring and is distilled via two of six stills incorporating boil balls, ensuring a light single malt. Glen Keith originally triple distilled to achieve a light spirit.

Without older expressions it is difficult to say whether or not at 10 years old this is the best age for Glen Keith. I feel however, that with a couple extra years in the wood this whisky will develop into something a little more like Longmorn although not quite as fruity.

GLEN KEITH 10 YEAR-OLD 43%

Nose	Soft heather & honey. A hint of banana.
Palate	Delicate, flat - one-dimensional. Light body.
Finish	Lovely, easy-to-swallow finish with a surge of honey as an aftertaste.
Comment	Uncomplicated, but wave after wave of honey in the finish. A very easy-to-drink whisky.
Style	B

Region *Speyside*

The second whisky boom began in the 1950's as world demand for blends grew after the rationing from the two great wars. Glen Keith was the first distillery to be built in response to the boom starting production in 1960. Situated at the bottom of the hill that Strathisla stands on and on the opposite side of the River Isla, Glen Keith was built on the site of an old oatmeal-milling factory. The Angus Milling Company was bought by Seagram's in 1957 who set about demolishing most of the old mill to make way for Glen Keith.

Glen Keith was originally set up to triple distil, perhaps to offer the Seagram blends an extra dimension (i.e. a lighter malt). This was abandoned in 1970 when two extra stills were added and a year later became the first distillery in Scotland to have gas-fired stills installed. This experiment lasted only three years before the stills were converted into steam coils.

Glen Keith was also one of the first distilleries to install computer software to run parts of the operation. The microprocessor was installed in 1980 and controlled the milling, mashing and eventually distilling. This allows Glen Keith to be managed by a small workforce and yet is still capable of producing twice as much spirit as Strathisla.

Glen Keith is set to change owners for the first time in a forty-year history. The new owners, Pernod Ricard, will be faced with a difficult decision as to the future of the distillery. While the spirit is of a very high quality, will it be a benefit to bring back production to Glen Keith, which has been silent for the past year.

Producer UDV Founded 1837

G lenkinchie is UDV's selection of a Lowland malt for their "The Classic Malts" range. Although a typical lowland malt is triple distilled, Glenkinchie is only distilled twice, however the two stills are very large and bulbous (wash still having a charge capacity of 21,500 litres) resulting in a typical lowland character

Considered by some as "Edinburgh's whisky" due to its close proximity to the capital city. Lying 15 miles south east of Edinburgh in Pencaitland in the Glen of Kinchie, the distillery nestles peacefully in arable farmland, which was once responsible for supplying over a hundred distilleries with barley.

Glenkinchie whisky is very drinkable with a full flavour and a delicious wave of smoke. This whisky is the greatest indicator that the regionality of whisky does not wash and it has to be noted that UDV deserve our thanks for making Glenkinchie the way they see fit. Who knows what may happen to the whisky if it was triple distilled, as is the tradition in the Lowlands. The whisky takes a good proportion of ex-sherry casks and this is evident in the soft sherry notes on the palate.

GLENKINCHIE 10 YEAR-OLD 43%

The Lowland representative in the Six Classic Malts.

Nose	Full on heather and honey. A soft, spicy follow through with brown sugar.
Palate	Heather mingles with soft sherry. The flavours combine well and a nice mouth-coating body.
Finish	The finish sticks to the side of the throat.
Comment	Quite a dry and heavy Lowlander!
Style	**D**

GLENKINCHIE 1986 DISTILLER'S EDITION 43%

Finished in Amontillado casks.

Nose	Grassy. Fruit wine notes. Crisp. Slightly nutty at first then much more nuttiness later.
Palate	Nutty and oily. Medium to heavy body and spiky.
Finish	Long creamy finish with a spiky aftertaste.
Comment	A good expression of Glenkinchie; full of side attractions.
Style	**D**

Region *Lowlands*

Two local farmers built the distillery in 1837 and farming features heavily in the distillery's history as Gordon Brown explains in his book "The Whisky Trails":

"In horse-and-cart days, majestic large-hoofed Clydesdales pulled the dray-carts at DCL distilleries all around the country. Those that worked in Glasgow used to be sent to Glenkinchie for their 'summer holidays', where they could canter and amble without the restriction of the carts. In the 1950's, the manager also ran the Glenkinchie beef herd that won the fastock Supreme Championship at Smithfield, Birmingham and Edinburgh... What an advertisement for the quality of the cattle feeds made from the malting and mashing process!"

Glenkinchie was originally called Milton as was Strathisla Distillery in Speyside, and perhaps confusion between the two distilleries led to the change of name in 1837. The distillery was later sold to a Mr Christie who showed no interest in the distilling side of the plant turning the distillery into a sawmill and a cowshed. This was not the fate for Glenkinchie and soon it fell into the hands of local investors before creating the Scottish Malt Distillers (SMD) with local distilleries Rosebank, St Magdalene, Grange and Clydesdale.

The SMD was ultimately swallowed up by the all-conquering Distillers Company Ltd that later became United Distillers & Vintners. Under the expansion programme of UDV Glenkinchie benefited from a visitors centre that was converted from the old malt barn.

Producer *Chivas Brothers* **Founded** *1817*

The Glenlivet's whisky has always been deemed light and floral and I cannot argue with this summation. Using unpeated malt and water from Josies Well, the spirit is produced via four sets of lantern shaped stills. Recent vintages have shown that The Glenlivet is an excellent maturing spirit. With age, The Glenlivet transforms into a deluxe drink that is so easy to swallow it should really carry a government health warning. At 12 years old, the standard bottling, The Glenlivet is still a big drink and is one of the best selling single malts in the world.

There is an obvious reason for the difference in taste between the 12 year-old expressions and the older expressions. The Glenlivet uses most of the ex-bourbon casks in their 12 year-old whisky, and the ex-sherry casks in the older expressions. The recent American and French oak finishes have tried, successfully, to give The Glenlivet advocates something to mull over. Everyone who has tried them has sung their praises and it seems these experiments are here to stay!

THE GLENLIVET 12 YEAR-OLD 40%

Nose	Malty, floral. Soft fruit flavours. Vanilla fudge. Toffee.
Palate	Bittersweet, creamy. Light to medium body.
Finish	Long finish with a nutty aftertaste.
Comment	A beautifully crafted whisky.
Style	B

THE GLENLIVET 12 YEAR-OLD FRENCH LIMOUSINE CASK FINISH 40%

Finished in brand new Limousine casks.

Nose	Heavy sweet oak. Spirity. Sharp. Wine notes and citrus.
Palate	Citrusy-sour. Light. Floral.
Finish	Bittersweet long finish.
Comment	It's Glenlivet but not as we know it. No trace of any vanilla from the new wood
Style	C

Region *Speyside*

THE GLENLIVET 12 YEAR-OLD AMERICAN OAK CASK FINISH 40%

Finished in brand new American casks.

Nose Caramel toffee. Vanilla. Fruit salad in Cointreau. Sweet mango.

Palate Fresh. Green. Bittersweet. Very light and crisp.

Finish Long oaky finish. No real aftertaste.

Comment The nose is astounding. Everything else is lying in the wake.

Style C

THE GLENLIVET 18 YEAR-OLD 43%

Nose Sweet sherry, light oak and a slightly grain spirit scent.

Palate Blood oranges, sherry and sweet oak.

Finish A spicy, warming finish that lingers elegantly.

Comment A more pleasant sweet oakiness emerges when left to breathe a while.

Style D

THE GLENLIVET 21 YEAR-OLD 43%

Nose Nettles, minty. Oaky. Creamy. Mulled wine spices.

Palate Minty, earthy. Very oaky. Light body.

Finish Long minty finish with an oaky aftertaste.

Comment This was the whisky that started my obsession. For that I must pay homage.

Style D

Region *Speyside*

GLENLIVET IT HAS CASTLES THREE,
DRUMIN, BLAIRFINDY AND DESKIE,
AND ALSO ONE DISTILLERY,
MORE FAMOUS THAN THE CASTLES THREE.

In the days before marketing and brand loyalty there were reputations. Reputations made or destroyed business and industries; they were the advertisements of their day. In the same way that Campbeltown was destroyed by whisky of ill repute, The Glenlivet's reputation made it the most sought after whisky. This was before, however, there was ever such a thing as The Glenlivet Distillery. The River Livet was awash with illicit distillers, over 200 at one time. The land became renowned for its quality of whisky, so much so, that royalty would request it (despite it being illegal).

George Smith was one such illicit distiller who was also a crofter on the Duke of Gordon's land. When the Duke pushed for the legalisation of distillers in 1824 it was likely that his influence over Smith forced/helped him to take out the first license. Fellow, illicit, distillers met this 'selling out' with some animosity. Threats were made, violence no doubt ensued and several attempts were made to burn down Smith's distillery. Eventually the Laird of Aberlour came to Smith's aid by giving him two hair-trigger pistols that Smith kept with him at all times and allegedly slept with them under his pillow.

The distillery was an instant success and Smith built a second distillery before scrapping both and settling at Minmore, the current location of The Glenlivet Distillery. Such was the reputation of the Glenlivet valley that distilleries as far away as Pitlochry were using the name, often including it as an afterthought to their own distillery name (for example, Macallan-Glenlivet). This obviously angered the Smith's who fought for the right to exclusively call their distillery Glenlivet. They only partly won their case allowing them to be the only distillery to be called The Glenlivet. Even today some distilleries still use the word Glenlivet on their packaging; old habits die-hard.

Producer Glenmorangie plc *Founded* 1843

The Tarlogie Spring supplies Glenmorangie with very hard water that contains no peat. The barley is very lightly peated and the eight stills have extremely tall necks (the tallest in Scotland) with boil bowls and pinched waists. The resulting spirit is therefore fairly light and is matured in ex-bourbon casks.

Glenmorangie is not the best selling malt in Scotland for nothing. The company's wood policy and vast array of expressions enables it to tailor a taste for everyone. Often quite delicate, the whisky has benefited rather than being overpowered by the casks used in finishing. Some of the rarer finishes have become instantly collectable and not because they are necessarily very rare. Glenmorangie is a drinking whisky and some of the finishes have been recognised as superb whiskies - collected for their uniqueness of taste rather than their investment worth.

GLENMORANGIE 10 YEAR-OLD 40%

This is the standard bottling of Glenmorangie.

Nose	Pear drops. Floral, buttery. Spices and lemon.
Palate	Gentle mouth feel, not too oily but still mouth coating.
Finish	A short, more-ish finish.
Comment	This is why Glenmorangie is No 1 in Scotland. At 10 years old it is hard to fault.
Style	C

GLENMORANGIE MILLENNIUM RESERVE 12 YEAR-OLD 40%

Nose	Oranges, spice. Sweet and buttery. Scented. Perfume.
Palate	A gentle sweetness. Malty and orangey.
Finish	Medium finish, very more-ish.
Comment	As good as the ten if not slightly better. A little more sweetness and oranges.
Style	C

Region Highlands

GLENMORANGIE CELLAR 13 43%

Exclusively taken from Cellar 13 and sold in Duty Free.

Nose	Apples, cinnamon, soft spice. Rice pudding - slightly citrusy.
Palate	Spiky yet soft and quite mellow. Stewed fruits.
Finish	Tingly, dry and coating.
Comment	A lovely, delicate expression of Glenmorangie. Delicious fruit in the finish.
Style	C

GLENMORANGIE 15 YEAR-OLD 43%

Released 2000

Nose	Caramel toffee. Fermenting apples. Soft oakiness. Cinnamon.
Palate	A dash of oranges. Light to medium body. Citrus sweet.
Finish	A delightfully long cinnamon and spice finish.
Comment	The nose has to be grabbed before it loses all the apples. Wonderful cinnamon finish.
Style	D

GLENMORANGIE 18 YEAR-OLD 43%

Nose	Soft heather and orange. Herbal. Honey.
Palate	Light-medium body. Subtle flavour. Honeyed.
Finish	Very long finish with aniseed aftertaste.
Comment	A more oaky flavour would be expected from the age, but it is not found, still soft and sweet.
Style	C

GLENMORANGIE TRADITIONAL 57%

Cask strength - to replicate the Glenmorangie made one hundred years ago.

Nose	Pear drops, lemons, gentle spice. Fruitcake - mulled wine.
Palate	Round, buttery, fruity.
Finish	Medium finish. Tongue tingling and fruity.
Comment	Another exemplary expression of Glenmorangie. The extra alcohol gives the whisky a nice kick.
Style	C

Region Highlands

GLENMORANGIE MADEIRA WOOD FINISH 43%

Glenmorangie finished in Madeira Drums.

Nose	Sweet wine notes. Grassy, herbal. Slightly buttery and spirity.
Palate	Soft, sweet - lovely balance of wine and spice flavours.
Finish	Long finish - no off notes.
Comment	At first taste a pleasant all-rounder. The finish is not as developed on the second tasting.

Style   C

GLENMORANGIE SHERRY WOOD FINISH 43%

Finished in dry Oloroso sherry casks.

Nose	Raisins. Sherry. Fruit cake, malty. Brandy butter.
Palate	Sweet sherry, medium bodied. Slight oakiness.
Finish	Bittersweet finish, acres long.
Comment	An excellent example of a finished whisky. The Glenmorangie is not attacked by the sherry, rather is complemented and graced by its presence.

Style   D

GLENMORANGIE PORT WOOD FINISH 43%

Finished in port pipes.

Nose	Rich, heavy, fruity. Slightly minty. Grassy and fresh.
Palate	Sweet malt and oak. Slightly spiky. Hints of spice.
Finish	Clinging. An oily, long finish.
Comment	The nose promises more than the palate delivers. The port pipe has totally transformed the Glenmorangie.

Style   F

Region Highlands

The biggest selling single malt in Scotland has for some time been pioneering developments in the whisky industry. The wood finishes and the careful selection of the casks has meant that Glenmorangie has been promoting its wine and sherry finishes long before other companies started dabbling with calvados and limousine casks.

Glenmorangie owns part of a forest in the Ozark Mountains of Missouri. The company seasons their wood by air-drying, rather than kilning, and then loan the finished casks to bourbon producers before shipping them to Tain. Glenmorangie malt whisky is matured in 100% ex-bourbon casks apart from the finishing whisky. There has been a spate of finishes from Glenmorangie in the last couple years including Fino, Tain L'Hermitage, Claret, Malaga and Côte de Nuits. When added to the more easily obtainable sherry, port and madeira finishes and the 10, 15 and 18 year-old expressions, Glenmorangie's range is the most impressive of any distillery.

Glenmorangie has an enviable policy of around 95% of all of its whisky being bottled as single malt, the rest going to their own blends. For most distilleries this percentage is reversed preventing the experimentation opportunities that Glenmorangie has.

At 26ft 3ins the stills are the tallest in Scotland and there is no doubting that the ex-gin stills with their 16ft 10¼ins slender necks help in creating the delicate balance in the whisky.

The distillery dates back to 1843 being converted from a brewery, although records date as far back as the 1730's. The older buildings of the current distillery date from the 1880's when the distillery was completely rebuilt due to being neglected.

The Glen of Tranquillity is an area of Scotland that often gets overlooked by tourists who either travel further north or stay south. The visit to Glenmorangie and the Dornoch Firth however, is warrant enough to trek out past the Black Isle into the little, unspoilt area where Glenmorangie has been distilling peacefully for the past 160 years.

Producer *Glenmorangie plc* ***Founded*** *1897*

A lightly peated malt, Glen Moray (Murray) utilise 4 onion shaped stills and matures its spirit in ex-bourbon casks. Some of the expressions are then finished for six months in ex-Chenin Blanc or Chardonnay wine casks.

Glen Moray was one of the first distilleries to finish their whiskies in white wine barrels. This has had a mixed response from consumers. Some have enjoyed the wine notes, expressing how subtle and compromising they are to the flavours of Glen Moray. Others, like myself, preferred the non-finished expressions.

Glen Moray is very competitively priced and that coupled with often superb packaging means it can be the first malt whisky that future advocates taste. I have yet to meet anyone who tried Glen Moray first and did not explore the malt whisky world further.

In the words of one whisky convert "it is refreshing to explore and find that there are other excellent malts apart from the regulars to be found on the shelves", "are you Scots keeping this one for yourselves"

GLEN MORAY FINISHED IN CHARDONNAY BARRELS *40%*

This whisky is 8 - 10 years old.

Nose	Strong new spirit aromas. Very young with definite wine and cereal notes.
Palate	Light and bittersweet with wine notes.
Finish	Chewy, dry aftertaste.
Comment	The Glen Moray style is evident in this classy dram.
Style	A

Region *speyside*

GLEN MORAY *12 YEAR-OLD FINISHED IN* CHENIN BLANC *BARRELS 40%*

Nose	Strong new spirit, spirity, cereal notes. Malty and slightly earthy.
Palate	Mellow, balanced malt and wine flavours. Light - medium bodied.
Finish	Medium. Slightly oaky. Pleasant.
Comment	Almost identical on the nose to the Chardonnay finish, although less wine input. Much more palatable - better balance and finish.
Style	A

GLEN MORAY *16 YEAR-OLD FINISHED IN* CHENIN BLANC *BARRELS 40%*

Nose	Spirity, cereal notes, buttery. Light and floral.
Palate	Malty, warming. Sweet oak and light - medium bodied.
Finish	A warm finish with an oaky aftertaste.
Comment	The extra four years has not changed the overall character much, although the extra oakiness is very agreeable!.
Style	A

Region Speyside

Glen Moray, like Glenmorangie, was converted from a brewery in 1897. Unfortunately it was built a year before the Pattison crash of 1898 and although riding that storm fairly well the distillery went into receivership in 1917 and was eventually put up for sale by the liquidator. Both Glen Moray and Glenmorangie were bought by Macdonald & Muir Ltd 1919. Since then Glen Moray has added two more stills taking its annual capacity to around 700,000 gallons a year.

Glen Moray has experienced relatively few years of non production and was one of the few distilleries allowed to continue producing during part of WW2. Since 1987 the distillery has been in full production, 24 hours a day, 7 days a week.

Glen Moray have released some port finished whisky from some 1976, 77, 78 and 79 distillations. Glen Moray was experimenting with wood finishes for its sister company Glenmorangie. In 1987 the whisky which had already been maturing 8 to 11 years in ex-bourbon casks was placed into port pipes and left to mature a further two years and then monitored to see what change if any took place. This was the test for the wood finishes that we now see on the shelves of our local stockists. Having spent an additional ten years in the port pipes the whisky was selected in 1997 to commemorate the centennial of Glen Moray.

Producer UDV Founded 1838

Flowing over granite and peat the water used for Glen Ord comes from the White Burn that contributes toward the lightly peated malt. Six stills and ex-bourbon or ex-sherry casks are employed to produce a malty spirit.

Glen Ord has for a long time been described as a malty whisky. It is hard to argue with this description on the current 12 year-old expression made available by UDV. Stocks of Glen Ord are becoming harder to find however and this may be a phase out programme from UDV. This will be the loss of what used to be one of the most heavily marketed malt whiskies on the market.

Some of the older expressions of Glen Ord whisky made available in the Rare Malts range by UDV have showed an oaky sweetness that combines with the malty flavours to leave a rather delicious, if a touch dry, expression of Glen Ord. As with many older cask strength whiskies, it is not for the squeamish tongue, but if battled reaps great rewards. If stocks of the 12 year-old dry up then we may see more vintage expressions being released. And as with all vintages each needs to be tried and tested as if it was a completely different whisky.

GLEN ORD 12 YEAR-OLD 40%

Nose   Malty and honey-sweet. Mild spices and heather. Slightly bitter.

Palate   Chewy malt and malt extract flavours. Light to medium body.

Finish   Medium finish, malty and firm.

Comment Without a doubt one of the maltiest drams on the market. A good example of what whisky might taste like if stripped of all other flavour giving variables.

Style   C

The Muir of Ord once boasted 10 licensed stills when Glen Ord Distillery was constructed in 1838. After a few financial mishaps the distillery passed on to a widow of the second owner of the distillery. She married Alexander McKenzie, a banker from Beauly who ran the distillery for ten years before selling out to James Watson & Co Blenders. The distillery again became a financial strain and was sold to John Dewar & Sons of Perth in 1923.

Dewar's later became a subsidiary of the DCL in 1925 transferring to the SMD in 1930. The distillery went under a programme of expansion and experimentation becoming one of the first DCL distilleries to convert their stills to steam heating. Despite all of the new technology the distillery gained it did not have electricity installed until 1949 and was previously being lit by paraffin lamps. Not the best practice in a distillery.

The distillery was completely rebuilt by 1966 and the number of stills was increased from two to six. Having had Saladin maltings installed in 1961 the distillery also had drum malting installed in 1968. This was to provide malt for the local DCL distilleries (of which there were plenty) and resulted in a capacity for around 600 tons of barley at a time. The factory-look of the distillery was complete with the construction of a dark grains plant that converts by-products into animal feed. In 1988 the distillery welcomed visitors opening a new visitor centre.

Producer *The Edrington Group* **Founded** *1878*

For too long Glenrothes had been hidden in the great blend Cutty Sark. Thankfully though the powers that be in Berry Bros & Rudd decided that the whisky was too good to hide and started bottling one of the best ranges the whisky world has ever seen.

Glenrothes Distillery was enlarged twice from four to six stills in 1963 and then from six to ten stills in 1980. Water from the bore holes on-site is used for distillation together with an unpeated malt and a mix of ex-bourbon and ex-sherry casks are used for maturation.

Everything about the packaging and taste of Glenrothes is classy, just like the head offices in St James' Street, London. The bottle is shaped like an enlarged grenade and the label looks straight out of a blending hall. Each bottle is labelled with just a few words describing the whisky inside and can present a brief insight into what you should expect. May I suggest however that, as is the case with any notes, you taste the whisky first and then read the notes.

GLENROTHES 1989 43%

Bottled in 2000.

Nose	Grassy, herbal. Sherry and aniseed. Bready. Slightly spirity.
Palate	Light-to-medium bodied. Sweet & sour, a touch oaky.
Finish	Delicious herbs and honey in the long finish.
Comment	Quite drinkable indeed.
Style	B

GLENROTHES 1973 43%

Bottled in 2000.

Nose	Sweet oak, sherry. Apricots, dried fruits - tangerines.
Palate	Rich, oily. No bitter or sharp notes. Excellent harmony.
Finish	Short, sweet finish. Tangerine aftertaste.
Comment	Much sweeter than the 1989. More oak input as was expected.
Style	F

Region *Speyside*

Many distilleries have strange locations, some isolated, some mingled with shop fronts and housing estates but Glenrothes Distillery wins the award for most striking location. Not the prettiest distillery in Scotland, Strathisla wins that, and not surrounded by the most beautiful scenery either as many distilleries are much better candidates for that award. No, Glenrothes is sat next to a graveyard. And not one of those modern easy to look at graveyards, the distillery sits next to the graveyard for the town of Rothes. If ever a distillery deserved to be haunted then Glenrothes is it.

Just by coincidence the distillery is rumoured to be haunted by the figure of 'Bye-way', an African that came over in 1894 as a small boy with Major James Grant of Glen Grant Distillery based in the same village. Biawa, as he was later called, became Major Grant's butler and was a well-known figure around Rothes. When Major Grant died he left provisions for Biawa with a room at Glen Grant House and meals at the local hotel. Biawa died in 1972 and was buried in Rothes cemetery adjacent to Glenrothes Distillery.

Glenrothes is the second malt distributed by Berry Bros & Rudd on behalf of The Edrington Group although it does not share all of the same confusing ties as Glengoyne. The whisky has been for a long time at the heart of the Cutty Sark blend and has only in the last 10 - 15 years been bottled as a single malt.

Glenrothes was built by a consortium of businessmen who were in partnership with the Macallan Distillery owners. Things turned sour as the economic situation of the industry dived and the company was forced into a merger with the Islay Distillery Co who owned Bunnahabhain Distillery. This merger formed the company Highland Distillers who in turn were bought by The Edrington Group in 1999.

⧫ GLEN SCOTIA ⧫

Producer Loch Lomond Distillers **Founded** *1832*

Both Springbank and Glen Scotia make a heavy whisky with bold flavours and it is likely that both need time to show their best. The current 14 year-old bottling of Glen Scotia is heavily caramelly and sherried. This may change with the new owners Loch Lomond Distillers looking to get a better portfolio of malts from their three distilleries.

Many expressions of Glen Scotia have a briny, seaside quality. This is better demonstrated in the single cask bottlings that appear from time to time from the independent bottlers. These bottlings may bear little resemblance to the standard 14 year-old as they may have been bottled from ex-bourbon casks and will show little richness and no sherry influence.

GLEN SCOTIA 14 YEAR-OLD 40%

Nose   Rich, resiny oak. Heavy malt flavours. Spirity. Sherry notes, raisins.

Palate   Caramelly. Sherried. Chewy. Medium to heavy body.

Finish   Medium finish - tongue-tingling. Tar aftertaste.

Comment   Robust and rich.

Style   **F**

Region Campbeltown

G len Scotia Distillery has shared a similar fate as Scapa Distillery. Indeed they were both once owned by Bloch Brothers in the 1930's and later Hiram Walker & Sons Ltd. They also shared similar location traits, albeit in opposite ends of Scotland. While Scapa was struggling to maintain a steady operation, workers from Highland Park Distillery were 'borrowed' to keep up stocks by distilling seasonally. A similar arrangement was made at Glen Scotia where employees of nearby Springbank Distillery would be 'borrowed' to keep the distillery alive and ticking.

Glen Scotia was built in 1832 by Stewart, Galbraith & Co who kept the license for the distillery until 1919 - a long time for the 19th Century. The distillery was then sold to the West Highland Malt Distilleries Ltd but this only lasted five years before Duncan MacCallum acquired it. Glen Scotia was silent from 1928 - 1933 and after MacCallum's death in 1930 the Bloch Brothers bought the distillery and operated it until 1954.

Glen Scotia changed hands a number of times before being purchased in 1994 by Loch Lomond Distillers who have restored the distillery and now have it running at full production.

Loch Lomond have perhaps bought more than just a distillery as Glen Scotia is rumoured to be haunted by Duncan MacCallum who committed suicide after losing a fortune in a business deal gone bad. Not that that is the cause for all of the recent silent periods - is it?

Producer *The Edrington Group* **Founded** *1775*

In the hills behind the distillery lies Loch Turret from where the water for distillation is sourced. Although this is a very well known distillery it is surprisingly small with only one pair of stills. A lightly peated malt is used and the whisky is matured in ex-bourbon and ex-sherry casks.

Glenturret, like Glenfarclas, is bottled at a number of different ages although the 21 year-old is becoming more difficult to find. With Glenturret however, it is quite clear that the older it gets, the better it gets. Of course you'll have to try all of them before you can agree/disagree with me. Life throws up these little posers from time to time!

Glenturret uses a good mix of ex-sherry and ex-bourbon casks to age their whisky although there is nothing overpowering in any of the expressions rather they let the whisky do the talking. This is a perfect whisky to demonstrate how one whisky can appeal to one consumer while not to another. Personally I would be very appreciative if I was offered any of the four expressions at almost any time of day.

GLENTURRET 12 YEAR-OLD 40%

Nose Grassy, faint hint of smoke. Cereals. Brandy-butter.

Palate Brandy-butter. Dry and medium bodied.

Finish An enormous resurgence of sweet oats.

Comment The nose is light but the palate and finish is all conquering.

Style B

GLENTURRET 15 YEAR-OLD 40%

Nose Perfumed. Spirity. Sweet peat and very creamy.

Palate Creamy, medium bodied.

Finish Long finish with a burnt toast aftertaste.

Comment Doesn't better the 12 year old.
The burnt toast finish is a surprise.

Style C

Region *Highlands*

GLENTURRET *18 YEAR-OLD 40%*

Nose	Perfumed. Cereal notes. Spiky. Spirity. Oaky.
Palate	Sweet oak, dessert wine. Light-to-medium body.
Finish	Short, sweet finish. No off-notes.
Comment	The three extra years has meant quite a difference. The palate and finish are very pleasurable.
Style	B

GLENTURRET *21 YEAR-OLD 40%*

Nose	Sweet, minty. Freshly cut lawn. Aniseed. Hint of smoke.
Palate	Light. Dessert-wine sweetness. Medium body.
Finish	Long, sweet, luxurious finish.
Comment	Again the three years has made a big difference - this time to the nose. Quite spectacular.
Style	D

Region *Highlands*

Acclaimed as being the oldest distillery in Scotland, Glenturret was one of the first to open its doors to the public in 1980. Records show that distillation was taking place on the same location as far back as 1717 but the Glenturret Distillery was founded in 1775 (the date that can be found embossed on all of the bottles).

The distillery lies between two hills, which allowed illegal distillers to post lookout points in case of appearances by the excise men. The distillery led a chequered career changing hands numerous times and distilling on and off until 1960 when it reached an output of 100,000 gallons per year. Glenturret is and has always been one of the smallest distilleries in Scotland. In 1887 when Alfred Barnard visited the distillery he recorded that it was capable of producing 90,000 gallons per year. Using the same number of stills (2) Glenturret haven't changed much in over 100 years. It is very inspiring to see a distillery that makes less in one year than some distilleries can in a month producing such a wide range of ages from twelve through to twenty-one and a liqueur.

What they have changed though has been applauded by some and scolded by others. With over 200,000 visitors a year Glenturret now boasts a restaurant, bar, coffee shop and gift shop. They are also about to open their "Famous Grouse Experience" which is set to be the worlds most innovative whisky experience. Through a range of interactive displays the attraction it is intended to be both educational and fun.

No report on Glenturret would be complete without mentioning Towser the ex-distillery cat. Towser reached fame by being included in the Guinness Book of World Records for catching 28,899 mice in its fourteen years of life. A statue of the cat can be found on the grounds of Glenturret - but who kept count?

Producer *The Edrington Group* ***Founded*** *1798*

Highland Park has been described as the 'Greatest all-rounder in the world of whisky' and it is not hard to tell why when you are drinking it. There seems to be a taste for everyone packed into any of the three common expressions. The gentle smokiness and sweet fruit make for an irresistible combination especially in the older versions. Malting one fifth of their own barley dried from locally cut peat on Hobbister Moss, this is a fairly peaty malt although considerably lighter than some of the Islay malts. The water comes from Cattie Maggie's Spring, with the spirit being distilled via two of four stills. All maturation takes place on Orkney within ex-bourbon and ex-sherry casks in their earthen floored warehousing. Highland Park has a heathery-smokiness that is not matched by any other distillery, probably, in the world.

It is almost irritating how near-perfect Highland Park's whisky is. I want desperately to find something wrong with it but only ever return to its subtleties and charm. My only complaint could be that it takes a few years to really reach its best. Not much of a complaint is it!

HIGHLAND PARK 12 YEAR-OLD 40%

Nose	Sweet smokiness combines with the sherry and malt. Scented. Undertones of heather.
Palate	Malty with delicate smoke. Sweet oak. Medium body.
Finish	A medium, peaty finish with a malty aftertaste.
Comment	If this isn't perfection then the next two expressions must be.
Style	E

Region *Islands*

HIGHLAND PARK 18 YEAR-OLD 43%

Nose	Dry sherry. Rich fruit. Soft hint of smoke, prune juice.
Palate	Immediate fruitiness followed by rich sherry and a delicious wave of smoke.
Finish	Long, smoky-sweet, sherry finish.
Comment	This is a monolith of a whisky. The soft smoke adds to the flavours in a cameo role that is so utterly delightful.
Style	F

HIGHLAND PARK 25 YEAR-OLD 53.5%

Nose	Rich, treacly. Christmas pudding. Brandy-butter. Spiky. Hint of peat. Marzipan and a hint of sherry.
Palate	So rich, taking hold of the tongue by storm. Christmas pudding and berry flavours. Sweet, heathery smoke.
Finish	A long, stewed fruits, sweet, luxurious finish.
Comment	Another monumental whisky. So rich and full of flavour. An absolute classic dram with so much depth and control it is quite breathtaking.
Style	F

Region Islands

Highland Park is the northernmost of all of Scotland's distilleries beating Scapa to the claim by a cat's whisker. The distillery is rumoured to have been founded by Magnus Eunson who was the local preacher and illicit distiller. It is far more likely that the distillery was founded by David Robertson in 1795, either way it is certainly one of the oldest distilleries in Scotland. Eunson was, according to legend, quite a cad and was constantly foiling the excise officers when they could make it to the Orkney Islands. Rumour has it that Eunson kept his maturing whisky under his pulpit in church and on one occasion hid his whisky in a coffin and spread the word that the deceased had suffered with smallpox. The deceased obviously hadn't consumed enough of Eunson's whisky!

Scandinavians may claim the right of being the first to bring distillation to the shores of Scotland (although the Irish may argue this), and if this was the case it almost certainly landed first in the Orkney Islands. Remains of the Norse past are scattered all over the islands as well as numerous historical sights such as Skara Brae and its stone circles predating Stonehenge.

Highland Park Distillery changed hands a number of times before being bought by James Grant in 1895. The Grant family held onto the distillery until 1935 when it was bought by Highland Distillers who owned it until the Edrington Group took over in 1999. Highland Park is still very traditional in its methods and operates floor maltings that provide about one-fifth of its malt requirements. Only the malt from the floor maltings is peated and yet the whisky is undeniably peaty. What stubborn stuff peat is!

Producer *Loch Lomond Distillery* **Founded** *1814*

It is quite obvious that Inchmurrin comes from the same distillery as Loch Lomond. Inchmurrin takes its name from the island shaped like a teardrop resting in the middle of Loch Lomond. The island presents an almost scale display of the local geography being situated on one of the many fault lines that run through Scotland. Not that this has any bearing on how the whisky might taste.

The original stills were of an unusual design, often mistakenly referred to as 'Lomond Stills' but are in fact pot stills with rectifying heads. Because of the unique design the distillery is able to produce a number of different malts. One of the facts that determine the character of the whisky produced is the physical length of the neck of the still. Generally the longer the neck the lighter and cleaner the spirit will be. Because of the design of the original stills, by varying the way the rectifying heads are utilised, it is possible to replicate the effect of virtually any length of neck.

The distillery now operates three pairs of stills with the third pair being of a traditional design, installed in 1999. Water is sourced via boreholes on site, the resulting spring water having no peat influence. A peated malt is used to produce Inchmurrin which is matured in ex-bourbon and ex-sherry casks.

Loch Lomond's ability to change the style of whisky made by altering the malt and stills used has not altered the overall style of the whisky too much. There is still a distinctive sea note that is not salty but definitely briny. Their cask policy of using almost entirely ex-bourbon has allowed the malt flavours to remain dominant.

INCHMURRIN 40%

Nose	Grainy. White wine notes. Sugar cane. Briny.
Palate	Oaky and oily. Light to medium body. Again briny.
Finish	Warming, medium finish.
Comment	Similar in many respects to Loch Lomond - slightly more grainy.
Style	B

Region *Highlands*

Loch Lomond distillery was established circa 1814 on a more northenly site to the present location which it now stands. Built here in 1966 behind a factory-outlet shopping area in the small town of Alexandria a few miles south of the shores of Loch Lomond. The distillery is workman like and not a picturesque little distillery one might expect from its name and association with the Bonnie Banks of Loch Lomond.

The distillery was converted from a dye works by the Littlemill Distillery Company who were at that time jointly owned by Duncan Thomas and Barton Brands of the USA. Barton Brands assumed control in 1971 before closing in 1984 under the name of Barton Distilling (Scotland). The distillery was bought by Alexander Bulloch owner at the time of A. Bulloch & Co, a wholesaler of wines, beers and spirits in Scotland.

Mr Bulloch had previously set up his own bottling company, Glen Catrine Bonded Warehouse Company and needed to secure stocks of maturing whisky for the warehouse. After the purchase of Loch Lomond, Mr Bulloch at the ripe old age of 65 set about increasing the capacity of Loch Lomond and installed grain stills. Having started with just two stills with a capacity of 500,000 litres of alcohol per year, Loch Lomond is now capable of making 12,500,000 litres of alcohol per year. 2,000,000 of that is single malt whisky, which is made in eight different expressions by altering the stills used.

Along with the other two malt whiskies commonly available (i.e. Loch Lomond and Rhosdhu), Loch Lomond Distillery Company also owns the Littlemill Distillery and Glen Scotia Distillery. Glen Scotia resumed distilling in May 1999 and Littlemill is expected to be in production in 2002. The company that like so many others had its routes in retail looks set to become quite a big player in the world of whisky.

Producers Kyndal Spirits **Founded** 1810

Jura was purposely re-built towards the end of the 1950's to produce a whisky that was closer to the popular Highland style. The stills were built large, 25ft 4ins making them the largest, although not the tallest in Scotland. Two were installed in 1963 followed by a further pair in 1978. The malt used has a very low phenolic level while the water is sourced from the Bhaille Mhardhaidh Spring which contains a high level of peat. Therefore although Jura is considered an unpeated malt, light peat notes can be detected through the soft delicate palate. Both ex-bourbon and ex-Sherry casks are used for maturation.

At the time Jura was rebuilt there was little interest worldwide in single malt whisky and particularly low demand for the heavily peated Islay whiskies. However, prior to being rebuilt, Jura ran much smaller stills and used a higher peat content. The two styles would have made for a very interesting comparison.

JURA 10 YEAR-OLD 40%

Nose	Malty, Flowery. Caramel notes. Green vegetables (Broccoli).
Palate	Sweet and malty. Medium bodied with undertones of sourdough bread.
Finish	Linger pleasantly on the palate.
Comment	In view of its unique location and individual character, Jura is very much in popular demand.
Style	C

JURA 16 YEAR-OLD 40%

Nose	Caramel, sherry-notes. Fruity. Madeira notes. Creamy and heather-honey.
Palate	Sweet, sherried. Slightly malty. Mellow and smooth.
Finish	Lingering, warming finish with a hint of mint.
Comment	Not sure if it is the extra six years that have made the difference or the extra sherry input. Perhaps both! A slight improvement on the 10 year-old
Style	C

Region Islands

The teardrop shaped island of Jura has more deer than its fair share. Jura is the Norse word for deer and these animals outnumber the human inhabitants making it a prime hunting ground - if you are into that kind of thing of course.

Once heavily populated, like its neighbour Hebridean island, Islay, Jura was devastated by the two great wars and many families who had lost their sons or fathers moved to the mainland to find work. Now there are only a few hundred people scattered about the island. However, in more recent times the island has played host to the writing of one of the most famous books ever written. George Orwell was resident on Jura while he was writing his epic 1984. To the locals he was referred to as Mr Blair and was somewhat of a recluse. Not that there is much to do on Jura.

In a remote harbour to the south of Jura, overlooking the picturesque bay and nestled below the paps (mountains) of Jura, the distillery has a most romantic setting. Jura was founded in 1810 at Craighouse, although it is believed that distillation on Jura dates back to 1502.

The distillery had a torrid history with high rates, problems with piers and eventually roofs being removed. That was until two Jura landowners; a Mr Fletcher and a Mr Riley-Smith decided to rebuild the distillery. This decision had more to do with repairing the worsening economic situation of the island than any other factor. With the help of William Delme-Evans, who had recently designed and built Tullibardine (and later Glenallachie) the distillery was rebuilt. Finally, in 1963 after battling the elements, the distillery began production of a lighter-style island whisky.

The distillery is now under the rule of Kyndal Spirits who formed a management buy out of JBB (Jim Beam Brands) in October 2001.

Producer UDV Founded 1898

D istilled using water from the Cardnach Spring and two of four stills this is a lightly peated malt. Knockando has been the heart of the J & B blend for a long time and as a single malt whisky fits into the same category as Benriach and neighbour An Cnoc. Knockando has received more attention as a single malt than both Benriach and An Cnoc put together and was for a while readily available. The interest in malt whiskies that has still yet to peak has done little for the reputation of Knockando.

It is possible that by bottling certain vintages consumers are wary about inconsistency although this does not appear to hamper Glen Rothes. It could be more that whereas Glen Rothes is a very individual and sometimes classic single malt, Knockando does not offer the same.

KNOCKANDO 1987 43%

Nose	Spirity. Hay. Background notes of sweet malt. Heather and honey. Fresh.
Palate	Salty at first then bittersweet. A bit watery but pleasant. Malty
Finish	Medium finish. Tingly hot.
Comment	Knockando will struggle to achieve cult status but works as a nice relaxing dram.
Style	B

Region Speyside

John Thompson, the builder of Knockando, could not have foreseen the Pattison crash that was to occur in December 1898, the year the distillery was built. This unfortunately meant that Thompson was unable to distil for great periods and eventually led to him selling out to W & A Gilbey in 1904 for £3,500. Gilbey's held onto the distillery for the next 52 years before being incorporated into IDV in 1962.

IDV was later taken over by Watney Mann who were themselves absorbed by Grand Metropolitan who would later merge with Guinness to form Diageo and the spirits subsidiary UDV. Throughout all of this change Knockando has remained the flagship for the J & B blend. J & B stands for Justerini & Brooks, wine merchants from London who were one of the first companies to advertise Scotch whisky.

The floor maltings were converted into warehousing in 1968 and a year later the distillery was rebuilt. Nowadays the distillery has function rooms and is quite often the hub of activity from visiting international agents and reps. Two Prime Ministers visited in the 20th Century, the last visit by Margaret Thatcher was to commemorate the one billionth bottle of J & B Rare to be bottled.

The distillery is situated in one of the most picturesque areas of Scotland on the banks of the River Spey. Surrounded by trees and foliage the distillery has stood proud for over a century. What began in troubled times being forced into small production runs has blossomed and is now a key ingredient of one of the world's biggest selling blends.

Producer UDV   *Founded* 1816

L agavulin (Lag a voolin) takes its water from a stream flowing from the Solan Lochs that are situated in the hills north of the distillery. This water has a very high peat content. Using four broad necked, pear shaped stills, and with steep lyne arms the resulting spirit is very heavy. The whisky is aged in predominantly ex-bourbon casks, save for the Distillers Edition that is finished in Pedro Ximenez sherry casks. Despite this the standard 16yo always reveals a delightful wave of sherry beneath the coursing peat. Lagavulin is by no means the most heavily peated whisky available (Longrow and Ardbeg are both higher in phenol content) but is not for the faint hearted either.

The Distiller's Edition has caused much debate in the whisky world. Has the powerful Pedro Ximenez casks tried to dominate the whisky? Or has the finishing allowed a greater balance of flavours? You can tell from my notes what I feel on the subject. For me the extra flavours and greater depth has created a whisky that is head and shoulders above the current 16 year-old expression. For the extra money it is certainly the better buy!

LAGAVULIN 16 YEAR-OLD 43%

The Islay representative of the Six Classics.

Nose	Instant smooth peat and dry sherry.
Palate	Wonderful infusion of sherry and dry peat. Quite a lubricating whisky!
Finish	A lingering salty finish with waves of dry smokiness.
Comment	A little two-dimensional on the nose but a triumphant finish.

Style   G

LAGAVULIN 1979 DISTILLER'S EDITION 43%

Finished in Pedro-Ximenez casks.

Nose	Waves of sweet peat and accompanying sherry notes. Fresh sea air. Smoky.
Palate	The wine notes and the peat slug it out with the wine notes winning the battle first before the peat makes a huge comeback. Heavy body.
Finish	Long peaty finish. Spiky.
Comment	Head and shoulders above the standard 16 year-old expression. Much to be admired and savoured.

Style   G

Region *Islay*

There are few sights more inspiring than the glimpsing of the first whitewashed walls of a distillery on the short ferry journey into Port Ellen, Isle of Islay. The second set of black letters glaring from warehouse walls is that of Lagavulin meaning 'mill in the hollow'. A powerhouse whisky that is as peaty as it is historical. Lagavulin or Lag A' Mhuillin, was established in 1816 and sits comfortably on Lagavulin Bay next to the 13th century Dunnyveg Castle, previously the abode for the Lord of the Isles. Although two pagodas are still in place Lagavulin no longer malts its own barley.

The ruins of Dunnyveg Castle are still visible from Lagavulin's short pier and it isn't hard to see why the castle was called 'bay of little ships'; the surrounding rockery being far too rugged for any large sea-going vessels to navigate. In the days before the pier was built, casks of whisky had to be floated out to the SS Pibroch, the puffer ship that carried the cargo to and from Islay and the mainland.

Records show that there was illicit distilling on the same site as present day Lagavulin as far back as 1742. Indeed when Alfred Barnard visited the distillery in 1887 he was informed that there were 'ten small and separate smuggling bothys for the manufacture of "moonlight", which when working presented anything but a true picture of "still life", and were all subsequently absorbed into one establishment, the whole work not making more than a few thousand gallons per annum.'

The current site of Lagavulin has been home to two other distilleries. At the same time the current distillery was being founded by a John Johstone a second distillery, assumed to be Kildalton Distillery was also built. Later on when Lagavulin came under the control of James Mackie (White Horse Distillers) another distillery was built by one of the controlling partners, Sir Peter Mackie.

Sir Peter decided to build Malt Mill Distillery and re-create a traditional Islay whisky (and also try and copy Laphroaig's style). He used traditional floor maltings and a hair-clothed kiln, which used 100% peat for the drying of the malted barley. What the whisky tasted like we shall never know as it was never recorded, but it must have been pretty fiery stuff. Malt Mill distilled for a further fifty-two years before becoming integrated with Lagavulin's plant in 1960 and then disappearing entirely in 1962. The malt barn is now the visitor's centre and the size allows you to see how big an operation Malt Mill was in its hey-day.

Producer *Allied Distillers* **Founded** *1815*

Yet again I am beginning to believe in the conspiracy theory. Has someone tampered with my Laphroaig? (La froyg). This was one of the first whiskies I tasted and I have possibly drunk what is medically termed 'too much' over my professional drinking career. I know Laphroaig almost like the back of my hand, or so I thought.

Malting its own barley with locally cut peat containing a high content of moss and using water from the Kilbride dam, Laphroaig used to be one of the most pungent whiskies available. The spirit is produced via two of seven stills then left to mature in ex-bourbon casks in one of eight coastal warehouses to absorb whatever the sea has to throw at it.

I have spent so much time with the three whiskies below to make sure I hadn't gone insane - you will understand when you read my tasting notes. I am not insane, just confused. What is supposed to be one of the world's most acquired tastes has gone soft - literally; full of the taste of dessert's and cocktails. I shall be trying a few more bottles of Laphroaig from different sources in the near future and if I find them to be of similar quality I shall buy all I can and recommend you to do the same. The 10 year-old (43%) and 15 year-old demonstrate a brand new taste and are two of the greatest whiskies it has been my utmost pleasure to drink.

The whisky is famous for its TCP, iodine flavours and even today is still viewed as the most extreme tasting whisky available. I beg to differ, if given time and certainly age Laphroaig turns into a complex, overly-satisfying dram that is not all about an antiseptic finish. I have highlighted the 10 and 15 year-old as two of my favourites and they would certainly be desert island drams. Even if you are not a lover of the peaty ones, don't knock it till you've given it time and then tried it!

LAPHROAIG **10** YEAR-OLD **43%**

Nose	Soft and gentle. Strawberry milkshake. Vanilla, roses and sweet peat.
Palate	Much more peat emerges. Sweet and briny like mussels.
Finish	Medium finish with a long smooth aftertaste of peat.
Comment	Ok, who's taken my monstrous Laphroaig and replaced it with one of the smoothest and most rewarding drams I have ever had the pleasure to drink?
Style	E

Region *Islay*

LAPHROAIG 10 YEAR-OLD CASK STRENGTH 57.3%

Nose   Overpowering peat and brine. Strong vanilla toffee and caramel. Crème Brule.

Palate   Delicious sweet peat courses over the tongue followed by a toffee sweetness.

Finish   Long peaty-peppery finish with a strong licorice aftertaste.

Comment   This is more like the Laphroaig I am used to drinking although ironically I prefer the standard 10 year-old. This one needs time to breath before the nose can take the strength!

Style   G

LAPHROAIG 15 YEAR-OLD 43%

Nose   Strawberries, roses. Sweet, minty peat. Hints of lavender and vanilla. Summer fruits.

Palate   Surprisingly soft and velvety with fruit flavours.

Finish   Medium finish with a lingering taste of toast.

Comment   The extra five years has done little but has removed some of the peat. This is still not the Laphroaig of yesteryear. Far too delicious.

Style   E

Region Islay

It is fitting that Laphroaig and Lagavulin sit side by side in the A-Z of malt whisky distilleries. The two distilleries are inextricably linked and their futures are as similar as their pasts. Laphroaig is older than Lagavulin by 1 year although that means nothing on paper as stills were firing on this stretch of land decades (if not centuries) before this.

Laphroaig was founded by Donald and Alex Johnston although Donald bought out his brother ten years later. His untimely death in 1847 was as farcical as it must have been painful. Falling into a vat of his own burnt ale is certainly always going to look suspicious when you work in a distillery.

Following the death of Donald Johnston the distillery was leased to a trustee of his estate who also happened to be the distiller at Lagavulin (helps when you are a stones throw from each other). This agreement lasted for sixty years until new owners decided that the original agreement was no longer fair. By this time Lagavulin was being run by the enigmatic Peter Mackie who was eventually taken to court over the matter.

Mackie was not known for hiding his views and shortly after the court case diverted the water away from Laphroaig thereby taking away their lifeline - another court case ensued. Mackie tried on a couple occasions to buy Laphroaig, unsuccessfully and it is believed that his experiments with the Malt Mill Distillery was to try and copy the Laphroaig whisky. As history has shown us, two distilleries never make the same whisky!

Laphroaig is thought to be Gaelic for 'beautiful hollow by the broad bay' and sits on the bay off the Laphroaig Loch. There was previously another distillery on the same site called Ardenistle, which operated from 1837 to 1842, but this was incorporated into Laphroaig. Established in 1815 the malting floors below the twin pagoda roof are still in use and are part of the original building. Laphroaig, for a while, was run by Bessie Williamson who had previously been the personal secretary of Ian Hunter. She was, for her time, the only female distiller in all of Scotland and was apparently an excellent manager.

Producer *Burn Stewart Distillers* **Founded** *1798*

Ledaig (Lay Check) is a glimpse into the previous existence of Tobermory Distillery. With a much greater peat content Ledaig shows much more of the seaside and some of the most interesting smells and flavours I have ever found in a glass. Until recently Ledaig was bottled in a series of vintages some of which are still available. These vary as does the current range almost as if the malting policy changed from year to year.

The barley is malted using a high level of peat and the water from the Mishnish Loch is also very peaty. The four bulbous stills have an unusual S shaped lyne pipe allowing only the lighter spirit to get through. Ex- whisky, ex-sherry and ex-bourbon casks are used to make Ledaig.

The 15 year-old expression is my choice but don't be too put off by the strange smells and tastes in the 20 year-old. Given a bit of time the smells will evaporate and you'll forget about the earthy tastes and the coffee, peaty flavours will appear. The 15 year-old needs no time to breathe as it explodes with delightful flavours and smells.

LEDAIG ORIGINAL 43%

Nose	Spirity and young. Briny. Smoked fish. A hint of sulphur and stewed vegetables.
Palate	Crisp. Peaty, tarry. Bittersweet and salty.
Finish	Medium finish with a long salty aftertaste.
Comment	Although no age is given there are some young casks in this vatting. Quite drinkable nonetheless.

Style   E

LEDAIG 15 YEAR-OLD 43%

Nose	Sweet and fruity with some sherry influence. Peat bonfire with heather honey. Hint of vanilla.
Palate	Dry and fruity. The bonfire flavours surge through. Medium body.
Finish	Medium finish with a lingering sweet potato flavour.
Comment	It is difficult to believe this came from the same distillery as the previous whisky. Much, MUCH better!

Style   G

Region *Islands*

LEDAIG **20** *YEAR-OLD* **40%**

Nose	Strong intense nose. Very earthy. Barley. Strong coffee notes.
Palate	Earthy. Stew. Sweet and slightly peaty. Heavy bodied.
Finish	Long finish with some extraordinary flavours left in the mouth. Fruit and raisins.
Comment	A most peculiar dram that needs time to breathe. Don't be too put off by the intense nose. Underneath all that hides a very interesting dram.
Style	E

Region Islands

Tobermory, like Oban, sits on the sea front of a small fishing bay. Unlike Oban the village of Tobermory was built before the distillery. Indeed the planning applications of John Sinclair were rejected a year before it is believed the distillery was built. The distillery was originally called Ledaig (pronounced Lay check) meaning 'safe haven' but with constant changes in ownership and silent periods it was inevitable that the distillery would change its name.

Sinclair kept the distillery in his name until 1837 and after changing hands a number of times fell under the control of the DCL. DCL kept the distillery operating from 1916 - 1930 and then mothballed the distillery removing much of the equipment. The distillery lay silent for forty-two years until it was revived, albeit naively, by Ledaig Distillery (Tobermory) Ltd. The acquisition was during a terrible recession and the consortium lasted only three years before closing Tobermory. Oddly enough the distillery was revived by the Kirkleavington Property Co of Cleckheaton, Yorkshire. Until this time production had been brief and often interrupted. When Burn Stewart acquired the distillery and all of the stock for £800,000 in 1993, production had only been carried out in eight of the previous 63 years!

Over the years the distillery has been used as a maturation house for Mull cheese and when Burn Stewart bought the distillery they were aware that warehousing would have be to carried out in Tobermory's sister distillery Deanston in Doune. This was due to the fact that the warehouses had been sold previously and turned into flats. I don't see what the problem is though, who wouldn't like a cask of whisky maturing in their front room?

Producer UDV Founded 1821

Some whiskies suit their homes with an almost eerie similarity. I suppose it is the same concept as pet owners beginning to look like their pets (well sort of). Linkwood whisky is as pretty as the distillery. Alas though neither the distillery nor the whisky receive much attention from their large owner and this is likely to remain the status quo.

There is nothing heavy or concentrated about Linkwood but every flavour is soft and delicate and even the bitterness on the palate does not dent the beauty of the whisky. Linkwood is favoured by most of the independent bottlers especially Gordon & MacPhail who have been bottling vintages for over sixty years. Some of these are untouchable but there is no need to spend the extra money buying an especially old vintage as the current Flora & Fauna is utterly drinkable.

LINKWOOD 12 YEAR-OLD 43%

Nose	Sour fruits. Salted butter and a hint of mint. Wheat. Pear drops.
Palate	Cerealy, slightly oaky and peppery.
Finish	Short finish but warming and peppery.
Comment	This whisky is like the string section in an orchestra. A very rewarding whisky.
Style	B

Region Speyside

L inkwood Distillery was built by a Peter Brown, an influential farmer of the early 19th Century. Brown named the distillery after Linkwood House, which was the Brown's family home. The distillery houses two units almost like two distilleries; this dates back to its expansion in 1971 when they increased their stills from two to six.

Peter Brown kept control of Linkwood until 1837 when James Walker took over. Walker had previously been the manager of Aberlour Distillery along with his brother John plus John and James Grant. Linkwood was rebuilt in 1872 and a further two times in 1962 and 1971. As a result of all of this rebuilding Linkwood became one of the prettiest distilleries in Scotland and should it be given a little more attention would probably become one of the most visited.

Many distilleries have famous characters in their histories but none more so than Roderick Mackenzie who was appointed the new manager after WWII. Mackenzie was fanatical and superstitious to the point of not allowing anything to be changed unless it was absolutely necessary - this included leaving cobwebs alone in the warehouses.

With the rebuilding of the distillery in 1962 and then again in 1971 the entire layout was changed and whatever Mackenzie's superstitions were died with him. The distillery is set out in a two-unit manner allowing the Victorian buildings to remain. Something that Mackenzie would have approved of!

Producer *Loch Lomond Distillers* **Founded** *1772*

As with Auchentoshan and Rosebank, Littlemill is true to the Lowland style offering a delicate whisky with light notes. This has nothing to do with triple distillation however as that stopped being the practice at Littlemill in the 1930's. So Littlemill should taste more like Glenkinchie but doesn't come close. To confuse matters further at one time Littlemill produced a heavy peaty whisky. Nothing can be taken for granted in this industry.

If and when the new owners get Littlemill distilling again the whisky they make will almost certainly be different from the stocks that are currently available. A lightly peated malt made with water from the Auchentorlie Burn, Littlemill was distilled via stills which had an aluminium outer skin and rectifying columns rather than swan necks. It is unlikely that Loch Lomond Distillers will fit new stills of the same shape. It is also unknown whether or not they will opt for triple distillation or not.

LITTLEMILL 8 YEAR-OLD 40%

Nose	Delicate spice and honey. Malty and perfumy. Slightly green.
Palate	Spicy. Nutty bitterness. Light and dry.
Finish	Medium finish with a beer-bitter after taste.
Comment	A stereotypical Lowland malt whisky; light fragrant and quite delicate.
Style	B

Region *Lowlands*

Littlemill is another claimant to being Scotland's oldest surviving distillery although it is not currently active. No one knows for certain whether Littlemill started life as a brewery or a distillery, either way there was an excise officer on site before the records for the distillery began in 1817.

The first recorded owners were Matthew Clark & Co although due to the economic situation of the whisky industry Clark only retained ownership of the distillery for one year. If Littlemill isn't the oldest distillery in the world then it certainly has a claim to having changed ownership the most times.

Littlemill was rebuilt in 1875 while under the ownership of William Hay until 1910 when the Yoker Distillery Co Ltd bought it. Littlemill Distillery remained a triple distilled whisky (as was the norm for Lowland Distilleries) until 1930 when it was under the control of the Littlemill Distillery Co Ltd. From there Littlemill passed onto Barton Brands and then Gibson International until they went bankrupt.

The distillery is now owned by Loch Lomond Distillers who have had quite grand plans for their distillery. Plans were afoot to turn Littlemill into a museum by 2002 but the cost of renovations and expected income from the venture made it unfeasible and there are rumours that Loch Lomond Distillers plan to restore Littlemill to bring it into production once again. One can only hope that this bold company succeeds!

Producer Loch Lomond Distillery **Founded** *1814*

The original stills were of an unusual design, often mistakenly referred to as 'Lomond Stills' but are in fact pot stills with rectifying heads. Because of the unique design the distillery is able to produce a number of different malts. One of the facts that determine the character of the whisky produced is the physical length of the neck of the still. Generally the longer the neck the lighter and cleaner the spirit will be. Because of the design of the original stills, by varying the way the rectifying heads are utilised, it is possible to replicate the effect of virtually any length of neck.

The distillery now operates three pairs of stills with the third pair being of a traditional design, installed in 1999. Water is sourced via boreholes on site, the resulting spring water having no peat influence. A peated malt is used to produce Loch Lomond which is matured in ex-bourbon and ex-sherry casks.

Loch Lomond is heavier and oilier than Inchmurrin and the sea notes and tastes are totally unexpected in the whisky.

LOCH LOMOND PURE MALT 40%

Nose	Malty. Honey. Mussels. Slightly oily.
Palate	Briny. Spicy and malty. Light and dry.
Finish	Short finish with a lingering seafood aftertaste.
Comment	The briny flavours will not appeal to every drinker but because of its uniqueness I like this whisky.
Style	**B**

Region *Highlands*

Loch Lomond distillery was established circa 1814 on a more northenly site to the present location which it now stands. Built here in 1966 behind a factory-outlet shopping area in the small town of Alexandria a few miles south of the shores of Loch Lomond. The distillery is workman like and not a picturesque little distillery one might expect from its name and association with the Bonnie Banks of Loch Lomond.

The distillery was converted from a dye works by the Littlemill Distillery Company who were at that time jointly owned by Duncan Thomas and Barton Brands of the USA. Barton Brands assumed control in 1971 before closing in 1984 under the name of Barton Distilling (Scotland). The distillery was bought by Alexander Bulloch owner at the time of A. Bulloch & Co, a wholesaler of wines, beers and spirits in Scotland.

Mr Bulloch had previously set up his own bottling company, Glen Catrine Bonded Warehouse Company and needed to secure stocks of maturing whisky for the warehouse. After the purchase of Loch Lomond, Mr Bulloch at the ripe old age of 65 set about increasing the capacity of Loch Lomond and installed grain stills. Having started with just two stills with a capacity of 500,000 litres of alcohol per year, Loch Lomond is now capable of making 12,500,000 litres of alcohol per year. 2,000,000 of that is single malt whisky, which is made in eight different expressions by altering the stills used.

Along with the other two malt whiskies commonly available (i.e. Rhosdhu and Inchmurrin), Loch Lomond Distillery Company also owns the Littlemill Distillery and Glen Scotia Distillery. Glen Scotia resumed distilling in May 1999 and Littlemill is expected to be in production in 2002. The company that like so many others had its routes in retail looks set to become quite a big player in the world of whisky.

Producer *Chivas Brothers* **Founded** *1894*

A contender for the greatest Speyside malt whisky, Longmorn has eight fairly small stills in which it distils a very lightly peated spirit with water from the Burnside Springs. Despite the attention it has received, it has not blossomed as well as it could. This is hopefully about to change with the take over by Pernod Ricard, who should be quietly pleased to have a chance to show Longmorn the attention it deserves.

Regardless of what happens in the future to Longmorn, the current 15 year-old expression available is quite simply superb. No part of the whisky can be blamed for letting the rest down and from the moment the aromas enter your nose to the moment that the fruity finish lingers no more in your throat Longmorn is a pleasure to drink. Under the control of Pernod Ricard this whisky could take off to huge proportions.

LONGMORN 15 YEAR-OLD 45%

Nose Sweet, round, sherried. Citrus fruits, perfume.
All perfectly balanced. Even a background maltiness.

Palate Explosion of fruit sweets resurging in wave after wave.

Finish Spiky, medium, fruity finish.

Comment One of the greats from Speyside. Delicious fruitiness from nose to finish.

Style D

Region Speyside

Longmorn, completed in 1895, was another distillery built by John Duff, albeit in partnership with George Thompson and Charles Shirres, operating as the Longmorn-Glenlivet Company. Duff had just finished building Glenlossie not more than a short walk west from Longmorn. The Rothes road that Longmorn lies adjacent to is now a distiller's row with distilleries on either side. The journey from Elgin to Rothes passes seven distilleries alone (not counting the further five distilleries in and around Rothes).

In 1898 Longmorn-Glenlivet took over Benriach-Glenlivet Distillery which is situated even closer than Glenlossie Distillery. Further mergers occurred when they amalgamated with Glenlivet and Glen Grant in 1970, who were then bought out by Seagram's in 1977 and finally by Pernod Ricard in 2001. Five years earlier Longmorn had been extended from four stills to six and later to eight stills in 1974.

The stills, like Glenfiddich, were split into two rooms; one room containing the traditional coal-fired stills and the other containing steam-heated stills as is the case at Glenfiddich today. All of the four wash stills were coal-fired in the first stillhouse while the spirit stills were steam fired in the second stillhouse. Since 1993, however, all of the coal-fired stills have been converted to steam heating. Longmorn also has one of the most impressive spirit safes, two or three times larger than an average distillery's.

Producer J&A Mitchell & Co Ltd Founded 1824

Springbank Distillery has the near-unique ability to produce several different malt whiskies all on one site (the only other distillery being Loch Lomond). Longrow is the heaviest of the three malt whiskies with a great depth of peat that neither Springbank nor Hazelburn share. This is due to the distillery malting 100% of its own barley, being kilned over burning peat for 55 hours and running the spirit through just two large stills. The original Longrow Distillery was founded in 1824 and closed for good in 1896. It is therefore only a revival of a name and perhaps an attempt to reconstruct what the whisky tasted like.

Longrow enjoys a huge cult status in the whisky world, as it is very difficult to get hold of and is highly sought after by collectors and imbibers alike. Earlier vintages of Longrow (from the mid seventies) have skyrocketed in value due to its reputation as a big whisky, and as the market shows, big whiskies are the 'in thing'.

Currently the two available bottlings allow you to really understand the impact that the sherry wood has on a peated whisky. I prefer the Longrow from the ex-bourbon casks as I find the peat is allowed an extra depth which is quashed by the sherry notes in the sherry wood bottling.

LONGROW 10 YEAR-OLD 46%

Matured entirely in ex-bourbon casks. Neither expression is chill-filtered.

Nose   Surging fresh peat. Almonds. A hint of maltiness. Sea breeze.

Palate   At first a sweet, honeyed maltiness. Then wave upon wave of peat.

Finish   The peat clings to the everlasting finish.

Comment   A taste of Islay from Campbeltown. The peat works well with the malty flavours.

Style   G

LONGROW 10 YEAR-OLD SHERRYWOOD 46%

Matured entirely in ex-sherry casks.

Nose   Spirity. Undertones of sherry beneath the dry peat. A touch of fruitiness and spices.

Palate   Dry sherry, subdued peat. Sweet and fruity. Heavy but not oily.

Finish   Fruity. A short finish with lots of sherry notes.

Comment   Nowhere near as peaty in the finish as the standard 10 year old Longrow. The sherry seems to bulge in the palate and dominate the senses.

Style   G

Region *Campbeltown*

Springbank is the most traditional of all of the Scottish distilleries. It is the only distillery that houses every part of the whisky making process including using local water before bottling. This allows Springbank to do pretty much what they want when they want and this ability to change rapidly to suit their own or their customers needs is rewarded with very high levels of consumer satisfaction. Despite Springbank's deliberate policy of running at less than 25% of its capacity, it is set to release numerous new expressions in the coming years, ensuring its popularity and desireability.

Currently there are three types of whisky being made (or maturing) at Springbank Distillery. There is of course Springbank which has slowly replaced its old bottlings with a 10 years-old expression in 2000. In 1997 the distillery triple-distilled a non-peated whisky called Hazelburn, named after another Campbeltown distillery, now lost. This whisky is expected to be bottled in 2006/7. The third type of whisky made at Springbank is Longrow, a heavily peated whisky that is distilled twice.

Springbank was founded in 1828 three years after the Mitchell's built their first legal distillery Riechlachan. The distillery is still in the same family's control and little has changed over the years after it was rebuilt in 1880. The Mitchell's are the saving grace for what used to be the busiest distilling area in Scotland. Over 32 distilleries once adorned the Mull of Kintyre and now only the Mitchell's and Loch Lomond with Glen Scotia keep it going.

There is only one other distillery clinging on to life in Campbeltown, Glen Scotia. In the past, employees of Springbank have been employed to work the stills in Glen Scotia thereby keeping stock levels up. Recent expansion has seen the purchase of Glengyle Distillery which should begin distilling again in five years time. The original Glengyle Distillery was built by William Mitchell a founding owner of Springbank Distillery. Glengyle Distillery is therefore returning to the family that built it over one hundred years later.

Producer The Edrington Group **Founded** 1824

The distillery with the smallest stills on speyside makes arguably the biggest whisky. Mentioning the word Macallan to a whisky drinker is akin to mouthing Rolls Royce to a car fanatic. Both words are the essence of luxury. But not only luxury, the words conjure up mouth-watering quality, finesse and style. To drink Macallan, to know Macallan, makes you somebody with taste.

Sourcing water 150 meters below ground via boreholes using a very lightly peated malt, Macallan distil via five large wash stills accompanied by 10 very small onion shaped spirit stills. The whisky is then left to mature in European red oak oloroso sherry butts within Macallan's climate controlled warehousing.

The greatest Macallan I have ever tasted came from an ex-bourbon barrel that had found its way to the Single Malt Whisky Society. This bottle showed all of the malty and slightly smoky character that is sometimes overshadowed by the sherry casks. Perhaps one day Macallan could let a batch get bottled that had never seen the insides of a sherry cask. Would the forefathers of Macallan turn in their graves?

MACALLAN 10 YEAR-OLD 40%

Nose	Malt, sherry, syrupy, heather and toast.
Palate	Lots of sherry, heavy and oily - quite a mouthful.
Finish	Medium, warming finish.
Comment	Deep, rich and almost sickly sweet. For the price and quality, this is up there with the best.
Style	D

MACALLAN 12 YEAR-OLD 43%

Nose	Sherry, fruitcake, syrup, brandy butter.
Palate	Sherry. A heavy whisky with superb balance and harmony of flavours.
Finish	Quite a dry, lingering finish.
Comment	The extra 2 years have made a world of difference. Defies its twelve years with insolence and charm all at the same time. Utterly delicious.
Style	F

Region Speyside

No. 6
LOW WINE
STILL

MACALLAN 1981, 18 YEAR-OLD 43%

Nose	Heavy sherry, molasses, treacle, Christmas pudding and fruitcake.
Palate	Syrup, treacle, brown sugar and molasses.
Finish	Powerful sweet sherry finish.
Comment	You really have to like your whisky heavily sherried and very rich to enjoy whiskies like this.
Style	F

MACALLAN 25 YEAR-OLD 43%

Nose	Oaky, rich sherry. Heavy spices. A hint of paprika. Stewed fruits that are a long way from being ripe.
Palate	Oaky richness and sweetness from the sherry flavours. Heavy and thick.
Finish	Heavy oak in the long finish.
Comment	This will be too much for some palates. Others however would pay twice as much for half the drink. Macallan certainly deserves its praise.
Style	F

Region Speyside

Macallan's claim to the throne as King of Scotch comes from their insistence on certain practices. Macallan matures in 100% ex-Oloroso sherry casks making it one of the heaviest and richest malt whiskies in the world. It also makes it one of the most expensive to produce. Macallan sources Spanish grown oak each year that is made into sherry butts in Jerez and then loaned to sherry bodegas for one year's fermentation and up to two years maturation of sherry. The casks are then shipped over to Speyside in one piece rather than being broken down into staves, as is the practice with ex-bourbon casks coming over from America.

All of this extra care and attention means that the casks used by Macallan are around five times more expensive than the ex-bourbon casks. On top of this, Macallan also use Golden Promise Barley for around 30% of their malting requirement. Golden Promise is now becoming very hard to find as it offers a low yield to farmers and distillers.

The Macallan distillers are a stubborn bunch but they do get the results from their insistence on high quality ingredients for their whisky. Presently consumer demand for the older expressions of Macallan is pushing the price of the stock through the roof and there looks to be no shortage of collectors and imbibers. Macallan is probably the most collected alcoholic brand name in the world and there is a network of collectors throughout the world.

The distillery is rumoured to be older than the 1824 date given as the first recorded distillation. It remained in private ownership until it was converted into a public company in 1966 to continue investment in the large stocks that were maturing in sherry butts. The distillery was slowly upgraded and each time demand exceeded supply the distillery invested in more small stills until it had reached 21 its current figure, though only 15 are currently in use.

The distillery is now owned by The Edrington Group who are as vigilant as ever in enforcing the ground rules set by earlier operators. The Macallan rarely lets the drinker down and in the two and a half years that Whisky Magazine has been published Macallan has never failed to win a recommendation (the only whisky to do so).

Producer UDV Founded 1824

A lightly peated malt made with spring water from the Conval Hills. Mortlach have six stills of differing sizes.

It's not often I struggle to find the right words to describe a whisky but Mortlach always leaves me one or two adjectives short. Perhaps there weren't meant to be words to describe some of the great whiskies or perhaps Mortlach is too good for words. That might be going a little too far but then this is a beautiful whisky.

When UDV were deciding which Speyside whisky should be the representative for the Six Classics it must have been with a heavy heart that Mortlach was not chosen. Cragganmore is a fine whisky and deserves its accolades but Mortlach is the choice for me. I have on a number of occasions named it as my desert island whisky and after trying it again it would certainly hurt a lot to leave it behind.

MORTLACH 16 YEAR-OLD 43%

Nose	Heavily sherried and fruity. Floral and perfumed. Spicy and quite complex.
Palate	Floral. Heavy sherry and fruit notes. Oily and chewy.
Finish	Medium bittersweet finish. Dried fruit aftertaste.
Comment	One of the greatest noses in the whisky world. Very complex making it difficult to pinpoint the flavours.
Style	F

Region Speyside

THERE IS A SAYING IN DUFFTOWN:

ROME WAS BUILT ON SEVEN HILLS, DUFFTOWN WAS BUILT ON SEVEN STILLS.

Although this is no longer true it certainly had been the case for the capital of malt distillation. Initially, after the creation of Mortlach in 1824, Glenfiddich, Balvenie, Convalmore, Parkmore, Dufftown and Glendullan all followed before the end of the 19th Century. After the closure of Parkmore in 1931, Arthur Bell & Sons, keeping alive the tradition, built Pittyvaich in 1975 next to the Dufftown Distillery. Ten years later Convalmore was closed and purchased by William Grant & Sons, owners of Glenfiddich and Balvenie who later built Kininvie on the same estate five years later.

Today however, Pittyvaich is no longer making single malt whisky and thus there are only six whisky distilleries in Dufftown. Pittyvaich is currently being dismantled and the dark grains plant has already been demolished.

Mortlach was built by James Findlater in 1824 and was named after the village and church that date back to AD 566. Mortlach had a hand or part to play in many of the local distilleries. William Grant who went on to build Glenfiddich served his apprenticeship at Mortlach. John & James Grant of Glen Grant bought Mortlach in 1832 and removed all of the equipment. The distillery lay idle for a few years save for the granary, which was used until an additional one was built in Dufftown.

Mortlach was revived in 1852 and was later owned by George Cowie & Son who kept the license for the distillery until 1992 as a subsidiary of John Walker & Sons of Kilmarnock. The distillery came under the rule of the DCL who owned John Walker & Sons in 1925 and was later licensed to UDV. The distillery was one of the few to remain distilling for most of WWII and bottlings from 1942 have been highly sought after.

Producer UDV *Founded* 1794

Within very close proximity to the sea, Oban is influenced by the salty sea air that makes its way over the pedestrian crossing and through the side entrance to the visitor centre. It is lightly peated and distilled in two fairly small broad necked stills. The spirit vapours are cooled using unique rectangular double worm-tub condensers then left to mature in ex-bourbon casks.

Oban has been chosen by UDV as its West Highlands representative for their " The Classic Malts" range. With its smooth and rich fruitiness together with a hint of dry saltiness and peaty smoke, it is considered a good balance between the Highland and the Islay styles.

OBAN 14 YEAR-OLD 43%

The Western Highlands representative in the Six Classics.

Nose	Heavily perfumed with a delightful mix of honey and malt throughout. Slightly spirity with a sprinkling of caramel.
Palate	A soft fruity malty flavour is the overall taste from Oban with a tiny hint of a sea breeze that coolly makes its way through the malt.
Finish	Long smooth and dry. A lingering aftertaste.
Comment	When left to breathe a while Oban turns into a little pot of honey.
Style	A

OBAN 1980 DISTILLER'S EDITION 43%

Finished in Montilla casks.

Nose	Heavy oil smells. Background brine. Creamy and fruity.
Palate	Heavy body. Peaty. Oily. Spiky.
Finish	Medium finish with an oily aftertaste.
Comment	What has happened to Oban? Much heavier and oilier than the standard 10 year-old but worth extra attention!
Style	F

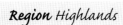

Region Highlands

Perched high on the hill is perhaps the oddest site in all of Scotland. No, not a monument to an Englishman, an even stranger sight than that; a coliseum. Built by a local philanthropic banker on top of the Creag a' Bharrain cliffs, the coliseum was constructed purely to give the local unemployed something to do at the turn of the last century. Perhaps this paradoxical picture subdues the oddness of Oban Distillery that sits below it squashed behind the sea front row of shops in Oban Bay.

The distillery outdates the town of Oban by several years being built in 1794 by the Stevenson's who were also partly responsible for building the fishing village Tobermory on the Isle of Mull. When Barnard visited in 1887 he described Oban Distillery as "quite enclosed, and built under a rock, which rises 400 feet, and is festooned with creepers and ivy. The water supply is from two lochs in Ardconnel, one mile above Oban." In typical Barnard form no clue is given to the taste of the malt. DCL (later to become UDV) purchased Oban in 1930 and the distillery was rebuilt in the 1960's and 1970's when the pagoda-roofed kiln was knocked down.

Behind the distillery at the foot of the cliff holding the already mentioned coliseum there lies a cave where Mesolithic remains were found dating from around 5,000 BC.

Oban means 'little bay of caves' although this has been bastardised over the centuries from its original title 'an ob'. Remains of a building were found when Oban increased the distillery warehouses. The cave is now sealed but the remains can be seen in the National Antiquities Museum, Edinburgh.

Oban is excellently situated as a stop before or after visiting Islay or travelling down to the Mull of Kintyre for the Campbeltown distilleries (all two of them, although only Springbank is open by appointment). From Oban you can also drive up to Fort William to visit Ben Nevis Distillery, which needs no appointment.

Producer *Kyndal Spirits* **Founded** *1824*

I have noted in my comment for Old Fettercairn 10 year-old that this whisky would make an excellent starter whisky. It is difficult to imagine what a starter whisky would be like due to everyone's tastes being different, but experience has shown me that often people who have not liked or tried whisky ask for something smooth and easy to swallow. Well Fettercairn certainly fits into this category.

However, the amount of times I have heard people say 'I was introduced to malt whisky by tasting a Laphroaig' or a similar heavy whisky, tells me that there will never be a perfect 'starter' whisky. Horses for courses as someone once said.

Using spring water from the Cairngorm mountains, Old Fettercairn is a lightly peated malt distilled via two of four rather tubby stills with straight necks and refluxes, then matured in ex-bourbon and ex-sherry casks.

The care and attention that JBB afforded their prized distilleries is evident at Jura, Dalmore and not least Fettercairn. There have, of late, been a few releases of independent bottlings that have astounded critics about the worth of Fettercairn whisky. Fettercairn gains richness and deep flavour when left in the oak. Some of the expressions could almost have been mistaken for a Dalmore. Hopefully with the formation of the new company, Kyndal, the future of Fettercairn will be an interesting one.

*OLD FETTERCAIRN **10** YEAR-OLD **40%***

Nose	Chewy malt. Spicy with a slight woodiness.
Palate	Bittersweet and light. Malty and oaky.
Finish	Short finish with a pleasant nutty aftertaste.
Comment	If there were such a thing as an ideal starter whisky Fettercairn would be an excellent candidate.
Style	B

Region Highlands

It seems certain that while Fettercairn was licensed in 1824, distilling by the proprietors had been carried out long before this on the slopes of Cairn o' Mount, one of the Grampian hills. When James Stewart was given the lease to distil on the lands of Sir Alexander Ramsay the new Fettercairn Distillery was built just a few miles away from the location of previous distillation.

The distillery changed hands a number of times and was rebuilt after a fire in 1887. Prior to this the Fettercairn Distillery Co had been formed with Sir John Gladstone as chairman. Sir John's son, William, later became Prime Minister and is responsible for the tax allowance relating to the Angel's Share. This was the first time that the government recognized the huge loss of spirit incurred by distilleries and brokers through evaporation. It has been said that William Gladstone PM was the first and last friend in the government for the whisky industry.

Fettercairn struggled to operate from the turn of the century suffering long periods of closure. After World War II the distillery regained operation and was expanded in 1966 with the addition of two more stills, doubling output. The Tomintoul-Glenlivet Co purchased Fettercairn Distillery in 1971 and was then bought by Scottish & Universal Investments Trust. In october 2001 this became part of the Kyndal Group.

Fettercairn is one of the few remaining distilleries in the east Highlands of Scotland. The closure of distilleries like Glencadam, North Port and Glenugie has left the east side bereft of distilling activity. Fettercairn Distillery seems to be in control of the situation however and even has a visitors centre. With the current owners the distillery certainly looks comfortable and hopefully the strength of their blends will secure the future of Fettercairn Distillery.

Producer *Inver House Distillers* **Founded** *1826*

Old Pulteney is the showpiece in the Inver House portfolio but for my money is completely overshadowed by Balblair. Older expressions have shown a greater peatiness and this seems to work better in the final product. With the current expression there just seems to be a bit lacking and I feel that it is the lack of peatiness letting the whisky down.

However, Old Pulteney is still a fine whisky and it must be noted that due to a little excellent marketing it is the top seller in a very famous whisky store in Edinburgh. This must mean there is something in Old Pulteney to please the masses. If you do come across some older versions especially the now rare 15 year-old sherry wood do not pass them by. They are hidden treasures!

Old Pultney use a pair of unusually shaped stills, the wash still having a large and bulbus boiling ball, the spirit still utilising a purifyer on the lyne arm resulting in a lighter spirit. Despite using an unpeated malt, it still has a peaty flavour which must come from Loch Yarrow its water source. The 12 year-old Pultney is mostly matured in ex-bourbon casks with some ex-sherry casks also being used.

OLD PULTENEY 12 YEAR-OLD 40%

Nose	Soft peat and malt - jelly sweetness with butterscotch.
Palate	Sweet caramel with a hint of peat.
Finish	Gentle finish.
Comment	Not as balanced as older versions. The peat just seems to be lacking a bit. A very fine whisky nonetheless
Style	**E**

Region *Highlands*

Sir William Pulteney built the town of Wick just 20 miles from John O'Groats, the most northern tip of mainland Scotland. Wick was a Royal Burgh in the 16th Century and probably enjoyed relatively peaceful times until the 19th Century herring industry explosion that brought thousands of boats, vying for space in the small bay. Pictures still exist at the distillery showing how concentrated the bay became - it was said that you could walk across the bay by stepping on the boats that lay huddled together.

With the masses came a boom in the entertainment industries and Wick eventually led the fight for prohibition becoming a dry town. Thankfully tours are now completed with a dram and no such idiocy exists as it does in the dry state of Tennessee where tours of the Jack Daniel's Distillery end with a free miniature - to be drunk elsewhere!

The distillery was built in 1826 by James Henderson, a long-time illicit distiller with about 30 years experience. The distillery remained in his family's control for nearly a century finally being bought by James Watson in 1920. Watson was in turn acquired by John Dewar & Sons but their control only lasted from 1923 to 1925 before the DCL took control and promptly closed the distillery five years later. Twenty-one years later Pulteney was revived by a lawyer from Banff who also owned Balblair. Four years later and the distillery changed hands yet again as Hiram Walker bought out Cumming in 1955 completely rebuilding the distillery in 1959. Currently the distillery is in the safe hands of Inver House Distillers who seem to make a point of buying distilleries that produce very drinkable, agreeable malts.

The distillery is rarely visited and this is perhaps why it was never conceived to build an aesthetically pleasing distillery. Like Oban and a few other distilleries it sits in a town and was never meant to be a place for sightseeing. However, tours are available if you should ever find yourself on the edge of Scotland with nothing to do!

Producer *Loch Lomond Distillery* **Founded** *1814*

The original stills were of an unusual design, often mistakenly referred to as 'Lomond Stills' but are in fact pot stills with rectifying heads. Because of the unique design the distillery is able to produce a number of different malts. One of the facts that determine the character of the whisky produced is the physical length of the neck of the still. Generally the longer the neck the lighter and cleaner the spirit will be. Because of the design of the original stills, by varying the way the rectifying heads are utilised, it is possible to replicate the effect of virtually any length of neck.

The distillery now operates three pairs of stills with the third pair being of a traditional design, installed in 1999. Water is sourced via boreholes on site, the resulting spring water having no peat influence. A peated malt is used to produce Old Rhosdhu which is matured in ex-bourbon and ex-sherry casks.

You are more likely to come across Rhosdhu in a miniature which is not the best way to sample whisky. 5cl is not enough to truly do a whisky justice, as it can be the third or fourth or even eighth time you try a whisky before you notice all of the subtleties and charms.

There are perhaps plans to bottle Rhosdhu as an older expression and this may allow the oak to do its magic and transform the whisky into something more complex.

OLD RHOSDHU 5 YEAR-OLD 40%

Nose	Malty. Popcorn and rice. Spiky. Grainy.
Palate	Crisp and dry. Grassy and nutty. Oily. Light.
Finish	Short finish.
Comment	A dram to enjoy by the Loch!.
Style	**B**

Region *Highlands*

L och Lomond distillery was established circa 1814 on a more northenly site to the present location which it now stands. Built here in 1966 behind a factory-outlet shopping area in the small town of Alexandria a few miles south of the shores of Loch Lomond. The distillery is workman like and not a picturesque little distillery one might expect from its name and association with the Bonnie Banks of Loch Lomond.

The distillery was converted from a dye works by the Littlemill Distillery Company who were at that time jointly owned by Duncan Thomas and Barton Brands of the USA. Barton Brands assumed control in 1971 before closing in 1984 under the name of Barton Distilling (Scotland). The distillery was bought by Alexander Bulloch owner at the time of A. Bulloch & Co, a wholesaler of wines, beers and spirits in Scotland.

Mr Bulloch had previously set up his own bottling company, Glen Catrine Bonded Warehouse Company and needed to secure stocks of maturing whisky for the warehouse. After the purchase of Loch Lomond, Mr Bulloch at the ripe old age of 65 set about increasing the capacity of Loch Lomond and installed grain stills. Having started with just two stills with a capacity of 500,000 litres of alcohol per year, Loch Lomond is now capable of making 12,500,000 litres of alcohol per year. 2,000,000 of that is single malt whisky, which is made in eight different expressions by altering the stills used.

Along with the other two malt whiskies commonly available (i.e. Loch Lomond and Inchmurrin), Loch Lomond Distillery Company also owns the Littlemill Distillery and Glen Scotia Distillery. Glen Scotia resumed distilling in May 1999 and Littlemill is expected to be in production in 2002. The company that like so many others had its routes in retail looks set to become quite a big player in the world of whisky.

Producer UDV *Founded* 1840

What should have been the most obvious choice for the Lowland representative in the Six Classics was upstaged by Glenkinchie, and is now mothballed. Rosebank Distillery sits next to a canal, and was no doubt built next to it for economic reasons in the first place. Using traditional Lowland methods of triple distillation with water from the Carron Valley Reservoir and aging in ex-sherry and ex-bourbon casks, Rosebank whisky is almost untouchable. Delicate, flowery and honeyed the whisky is everything a Lowland whisky should be and thankfully there are still vast stocks available.

ROSEBANK 12 YEAR-OLD 43%

Nose	Light and floral. Slightly grassy and oily. A touch spirity. Hint of sweet berries.
Palate	Sweet and gentle. Floral. Light but oily.
Finish	Long finish with just a hint of oakiness.
Comment	A great whisky that will be sadly missed.
Style	A

Region Lowlands

Rosebank is thought to have been constructed in part of the Camelon Distillery which occupied the same site as Rosebank does today. Records show that the Camelon Distillery was around at least fourteen years before Rosebank emerged in 1840. Either Rosebank incorporated the Camelon maltings into its own buildings or was constructed on the site of Camelon's maltings. Either way there was a period where both distilleries were working at the same time as Camelon closed in 1968 and later demolished.

Rosebank was built by James Rankine then taken over by his son who continued to modernise the distillery. Eventually the distillery was rebuilt in 1865 straddling the new road as it meant that farmers' wagons could directly access the top-floor barley loft. The whisky was highly sought after and annual production peaked at 123,000 gallons per year. Demand was so high for Rosebank whisky that Rankine was able to charge his customers warehouse rent; he was the only one at that time able to do so.

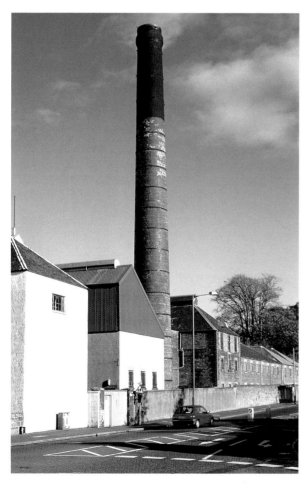

Rosebank was one of the original founders of the Scottish Malt Distillers along with Glenkinchie, St Magdalene, Grange and Clydesdale. Of the five only Glenkinchie survives. Rosebank was closed in 1993 and although it was deemed a difficult decision by DCL at the time in the current climate of astonishing growth in the single malt market it doesn't look like UDV (the current owners) are prepared to get Rosebank up and running again. If someone doesn't come along and buy it soon we may be drinking the last of Rosebank.

Producer UDV *Founded* 1826

A lightly peated whisky, sourcing its water from a nearby peaty dam. Two short stills are used to distil Royal Lochnagar which is then passed through a cast iron worm-tub before being left to mature in ex-bourbon and ex-sherry casks.

As a small distillery, Royal Lochnagar does share a few similarities with Edradour of old. It bares no resemblance to the current Edradour expression though this is partly due to most of the Lochnagar whisky aged in sherry casks being saved for the Selected Reserve. This whisky which takes the most exceptional casks selected by the manager can contain some very old casks; priced at over £175 you should expect nothing less.

The 12 year-old Lochnagar is a novelty whisky, yet it is fairly hard to find, which is shame as it is a pleasant whisky. It would be interesting to find out what Lochnagar tasted like in Begg's day and to determine just how awful a glass of claret laced with Lochnagar would taste (see the distillery notes).

ROYAL LOCHNAGAR 12 YEAR-OLD **40%**

Nose	Malt and honey. Heather and mild spices. Slightly soapy. Mint.
Palate	Quite watery. More mild spice and mint. Light to medium body.
Finish	Medium finish.
Comment	Malty and honey - can't imagine it tasting good when mixed with claret!.
Style	C

Region Highlands

Lochnagar is one of only three distilleries to use the 'Royal' title; the others being Glenury-Royal and Royal Brackla (Glenury was demolished and Brackla is currently mothballed). The warrant was awarded shortly after Queen Victoria and her family visited Lochnagar. They had recently purchased Balmoral Estate as their Highland escape. Victoria is said to have laced her claret with Lochnagar whisky, and as one journalist put it 'ruined both the drinks'.

Lochnagar was founded in 1826 by James Robertson who was formerly an illicit distiller on the same estate. The distillery was kept under Robertson's control until it was destroyed by fire and later rebuilt by Alexander Farquharson & Reid licensees in 1942. The current distillery however was built by John Begg on the south side of the River Dee. This distillery was called New Lochnagar until it was given the Royal Warrant. The original Lochnagar closed in 1860 and was eventually passed on to Begg.

The distillery was rebuilt in 1906 and was acquired by John Dewar & Sons ten years later before passing onto the DCL in 1925. Throughout its changes the distillery has remained one of the smallest in Scotland and is immaculately kept. It is a wonder that it was not inducted into the Six Classics range, although this is probably due to the annual output of the distillery. In 1990 the distillery converted the farmstead into a visitors centre and despite its unique location receives a fair number of visitors each year.

Producer *Allied Distillers* **Founded** *1885*

As if to second my motion that regions are not appropriate for categorising whisky, Scapa and Highland Park show how different a neighbouring distillery can be. Granted that Scapa Distillery uses water from the Lingro Burn and a Lomond still that gives a heavy, oily spirit, but even so the whiskies are totally different. Scapa like Caol Ila and many other good single malts get better coverage from the independent bottlers. Currently Gordon & MacPhail of Elgin bottle several expressions of Scapa but none are better than the Allied bottling.

Despite the fact that little or no peat is used to produce the malted barley, the Scapa 12 year-old is a heavy affair indeed. The heavy spirit must be the result of the Lomond still used complimented by the very peaty water. There is a delightful hint of seaside on the nose but also distinctive sherry note followed by a very sweet palate despite the fact that Scape only use ex-bourbon casks for maturation!

SCAPA 12 YEAR-OLD 40%

Nose	Heavily sherried. Fruity. Just a hint of the seaside. Honeycomb.
Palate	Bucket loads of honey followed by a fruit cocktail. Medium body.
Finish	Short finish with a bittersweet aftertaste.
Comment	A very respectable dram worlds apart from its neighbour Highland Park.
Style	F

Region Islands

Like Deanston Distillery in Doune, Scapa Distillery is doomed to be overshadowed by a local spot of historical interest; the Scapa Flow, which holds the German fleet, scuttled on the orders of von Reuter who was allegedly fed up with the post-war repatriation negotiations. Unlike Deanston however, the visitors to Scapa Flow will often discover, to their delight, that there is a distillery with the same name. Tourists are odd people!

Scapa was built in 1885 by Macfarlane and Townsend but this partnership was dissolved two years later when J. Townsend continued the business before selling to the Scapa Distillery Co Ltd in 1919. This consortium was liquidated in 1936 and the distillery was acquired by the Bloch Brothers who also owned Glen Scotia in Campbeltown. Eventually Scapa was sold to Hiram Walker & Sons in 1954. The distillery under Hiram Walkers reign was rebuilt five years later when a Lomond still was installed.

Allied are now the owners of Scapa and despite help from the operators of Highland Park Distillery that lies half a mile north of Scapa, the distillery is treading on thin ice. History has shown us that Allied have a habit of neglecting and closing very decent distilleries that would certainly blossom under a different company's management. Stocks of Scapa whisky are still very high and independent bottlings are almost countless. This state should last another decade but what happens to Scapa in the meantime is anyone's guess.

Producer *Inver House Distillers* **Founded** *1897*

Speyburn is the maltiest expression to come from Inver House although not the tastiest by any stretch of the imagination. Inver House seem to acquire distilleries in pairs whether by choice or default. Balblair and Old Pulteney are similar malts as are An Cnoc and Speyburn. What help this gives the company remains to be seen, but as a range of malt whiskies it offers little variation to the consumer.

Speyburn have a single pair of stills and use water from the Granty burn for distillation.

There have been a number of older expressions of Speyburn made available and these have scored very well in tastings but they are few and far between. Perhaps if Speyburn were given a little more time in the cask the whisky would lose some of the chalkiness that lets the whisky down.

*SPEYBURN **10** YEAR-OLD **40%***

Nose	Incredibly malty. Chalky and dry grass - very earthy.
Palate	Malty and very bittersweet. Light to medium body.
Finish	Tingly, warming finish.
Comment	Quite pungent and very earthy on the nose. For those who like their whisky malty and grassy.
Style	C

Region *Speyside*

Speyburn rests peacefully on the side of a hill in what is one of the prettiest areas of Scotland. The area in the Glen of Rothes is very steep and meant that the distillery had to be built upwards and on two floors. The area was once known as the Gibbet as it was the area for execution of local criminals.

Speyburn was another in a long list of distilleries designed by Charles Doig, the most eminent distillery architect and inventor of his day (and really of any day). His part in the design of Speyburn almost guaranteed pagoda roofs, his trademark design for the tops of the malt kilns.

Speyburn was built in 1897 by the Speyburn-Glenlivet Company, a subsidiary of John Hopkins, who were themselves bought by the DCL in 1916 during the whisky depression period following the Pattison crash. The first whisky was rushed off the stills in order to have maturing stocks to mark the diamond jubilee of Queen Victoria. This was done in such haste that the still house doors and windows were not constructed and work was conducted in the middle of a snowstorm. The distillery was silent 1930-1934 and John Hopkins' company was liquidated in 1962 and the distillery then transferred to the Scottish Malt Distillers.

Not the most exciting history of any of the distilleries but Speyside did become the first distillery to have drum maltings installed, using rotating cylinders instead of the traditional floor maltings. These were closed in 1968 and the distillery was sold to Inver House in 1991.

Producer *Speyside Distillery Company* **Founded** *1991*

This book happens to be written at an ideal time for Speyside as it takes around ten years for the first real results to be seen from the creation of a distillery. As the first spirit ran off the stills in December 1990 the staff at Speyside have been waiting patiently for their spirit to come of age. And so it is my pleasure to unveil the Speyside 10 year-old single malt whisky.

Of course there has been a whisky available from this distillery for a few years now. Drumguish is around 5 years old and is a much maltier dram than Speyside. It is quite remarkable to taste them in one sitting and see what five years can do for a whisky. They could be from the opposite sides of the world.

Speyside is a light peated malt, distilled with spring water from the Gaick Deer Estate.

SPEYSIDE *10* YEAR-OLD *40%*

Nose	Dried wheat heaped with honey. Oatmeal, biscuits. Hint of sherry.
Palate	Only shades of what is promised on the nose. Biscuity and honeyed.
Finish	Medium finish with some honey tastes.
Comment	Completely different from Drumguish. More refined but has lost most of the malty flavours.
Style	C

Region *Highlands*

Speyside is the second youngest distillery in Scotland and is a dream-come-true for George Christie. Christie started to fulfil his dream back in 1955 when he formed the Speyside Distillery & Bonding Co. A year later the distillery site was acquired near Kingussie at Drumguish, the name given to the first malt whisky bottled by the company. The building of the distillery began in 1962; an extension was built in 1980 but it wasn't until 1987 that the distillery was completed.

It took another three years before the first spirit ran from the two pot stills on December 12 1990. The distillery had taken the best part of four decades to complete and finally now in 2002 the company has what it desperately wanted; it's own 10 year-old single malt whisky. Anyone thinking of building their own distillery should sit up and take notice.

The current Speyside Distillery is named after a previous Speyside Distillery that was also situated in Kingussie. The former distillery was built in 1895 although it only survived until 1911 when it was subsequently dismantled and demolished. The current distillery sits near the A9 that runs through the middle of central Scotland which means despite its name the whisky is not a Speyside whisky.

Producer J&A Mitchell & Co Ltd *Founded* 1828

Springbank can truly claim to be the genuine article with its insistance to not chill-filtering its malt or adding colourings. Springbank malts 100% of its own barley with the springbank malt spending just six hours over smouldering peat. The spirit is made using spring water from the Crosshill Loch, and direct flame is used to heat the wash still, believing the charring effects the flavour. The spirit is distilled two and half times through three broad necked stills resulting in a medium peated malt. Springbank is matured in both ex-bourbon and ex-sherry casks and some experimentation with rum casks is being carried out.

Advocates of Springbank are keen to point out that the 21 year-old expression is the best although stocks of this age are drying up and may be discontinued. Very old bottles of Springbank can be found scattered throughout the world and it is really with age that Springbank begins to shine.

Whenever drinking Springbank it is essential that the whisky be given time to breathe. After a few minutes the whisky will begin to show what lies beneath.

SPRINGBANK *10* YEAR-OLD *46%*

Nose	Spirity, orangey. Hint of dry peat. Yeasty. Fresh and grassy. Slightly minty.
Palate	Dry, grassy - medium bodied. Oily.
Finish	Earthy, peaty finish.
Comment	Shows much promise and developing complexity. The older it gets, the better it gets.

Style   E

Region Campbeltown

Springbank is the most traditional of all of the Scottish distilleries. It is the only distillery that houses every part of the whisky making process including using local water before bottling. This allows Springbank to do pretty much what they want when they want and this ability to change rapidly to suit their own or their customers needs is rewarded with very high levels of consumer satisfaction. Despite Springbank's deliberate policy of running at less than 25% of its capacity, it is set to release numerous new expressions in the coming years, ensuring its popularity and desireability.

Currently there are three types of whisky being made (or maturing) at Springbank Distillery. There is of course Springbank which has slowly replaced its old bottlings with a 10 year-old expression in 2000. In 1997 the distillery triple-distilled a non-peated whisky called Hazelburn, named after another Campbeltown distillery, now lost. This whisky is expected to be bottled in 2006/7. The third type of whisky made at Springbank is Longrow, a heavily peated whisky that is distilled twice.

Springbank was founded in 1828 three years after the Mitchell's built their first legal distillery Riechlachan. The distillery is still in the same family's control and little has changed over the years after it was rebuilt in 1880. The Mitchell's are the saving grace for what used to be the busiest distilling area in Scotland. Over 32 distilleries once adorned the Mull of Kintyre and now only the Mitchell's and Loch Lomond with Glen Scotia keep it going.

There is only one other distillery clinging on to life in Campbeltown, Glen Scotia. In the past, employees of Springbank have been employed to work the stills in Glen Scotia thereby keeping stock levels up. Recent expansion has seen the purchase of Glengyle Distillery which should begin distilling again in five years time. The original Glengyle Distillery was built by William Mitchell a founding owner of Springbank Distillery. Glengyle Distillery is therefore returning to the family that built it over one hundred years later.

Producer Chivas Brothers **Founded** 1786

As an unpeated malt using 2 lantern shaped wash stills and 2 spirit stills with boil balls, Strathisla is a light whisky made with water from the Fons Bullions Springs conveniently situated on site. Maturation takes place in ex-bourbon or ex-sherry casks.

Strathisla has been the heart of the Chivas Regal blend since its acquisition by the Chivas Bros in 1950. This is a pleasant whisky although nothing grabs the imbibers attention and hence the reason for its success as part of a blend.

Assuming the flagging fortunes of Chivas Regal take a turn for the better, under new owners Pernod Ricard, Strathisla will no doubt continue production and we will continue to see Strathisla single malt for sale. If Chivas Regal does not regain market share then things could turn for the worse for the prettiest distillery in Scotland.

Occasional bottlings of Strathisla are released by the independents but for a long time Gordon & MacPhail have cornered the market for Strathisla lovers. Some of the bottlings of late have been extremely old and have delivered much to sing and dance about. Often however the whiskies have been swamped by the input of the oak casks. If Pernod Ricard do wish to take advantage of this delightful distillery they may wish to check their stocks for some cracking vintages. Can't let Gordon & MacPhail have all the fun!

STRATHISLA 12 YEAR-OLD 43%

Nose	Fennel. Creamy, spicy. Brown bread. Nutmeg.
Palate	Spiky, medium bodied. Burnt toast. Not sweet or too bitter.
Finish	Long, tingly, spiky finish.
Comment	All round very pleasing. Nothing shocks the drinker into submission but very drinkable.
Style	C

Region Speyside

Strathisla was originally known as The Milton Distillery taking its water from the Fons Bulliens Well (fed by the Broomhill Spring). Built originally in 1786 by George Taylor, Strathisla is one of the oldest distilleries in Scotland (only Glenturret, Littlemill and Bowmore can claim to be older). After George Taylor's reign The Milton Distillery went into the ownership of William Longmore who became the town's philanthropist building a town hall, a bowling green and fixing the church bell of Newhill.

William Longmore will be remembered more for his work on the distillery than his generosity. The work was pre-empted twice by two fires, the first of which was on 22 January 1876. 30 cows died in the fire (at a loss of £700 along with 500 quarters of barley) - the fire did not interfere with the operations and although the damage was a staggering £3,800 it appears that none of the whisky was caught - so no explosions.

William Longmore left the distillery to be run by his son-in-law John Geddes-Brown who in-turn set up William Longmore & Company offering 7000 shares at £5 each. In 1850 Milton was renamed Strathisla, meaning the Valley of Isla but then reverted to Milton-Keith in 1870. It was not until 1880 that the distillery reverted back to the name Strathisla although you may still hear some of the older locals still referring to it as the Milton Distillery.

Strathisla Distillery is one of the few distilleries being able to claim an almost perfect distilling history. Since its legalisation in 1824 it has only stopped distilling once when all distilling was terminated as World War II took it's toll on British industry. However this near perfect distilling history was chequered when a Mr Jay Pomeroy, a financier from London, took control of William Longmore & Co.

Mr Pomeroy's ability was not in distilling as he was once quoted as saying "…I may not know much about whisky, but I can tell you one or two things about finance!" His ability was in tax evasion and having bought out the majority of shares for the distillery proceeded to cut off all business with locals and sent all of the whisky to London where it is believed it was bottled under spurious names and sold on the black market.

Thankfully for The Milton Distillery, Mr James Barclay on the orders of Chivas Brothers purchased the distillery in 1950 and all sides of the business returned to normal and legal. The distillery today encapsulates all of the romance and mysticism that surrounds Scotch whisky. With its pretty water-wheel and twin pagodas this is a perfect distillery to visit with self guided tours and a luxurious visitors centre and shop.

Producer UDV   Founded 1831

Much has been written about the taste of Talisker. The whisky has enjoyed a long tradition of admirers including such notable figures as Robert Louis Stevenson and Derek Cooper. It is indeed a bold, fiery and warming spirit that almost has the right to claim it's own region. It is a whisky that so many people return to as if it was an old friend they have missed. Perhaps Talisker and only Talisker can claim brand loyalty like no other whisky.

Soft spring water from Hawk Hill together with medium peated malt is used to produce Talisker, which may come as a surprise since there is a distinct peatyness on the nose and palate. The spirit is distilled through two of five relatively small, slender necked stills, although prior to 1928 Talisker was triple distilled. The stills are now fitted with rectifiers which together with the longer than usual 60-hour fermentation process help produce a light clean spirit.

Talisker is predominantly matured in ex-bourbon casks, with the Distillers Edition being further matured in Amoroso casks. Amoroso is a sweet wine from Spain.

The release of the Distiller's Edition Talisker was waited for with baited breath by advocates the world over anxious to see if this giant whisky could be bettered through finishing. Almost as a relief, I do not think Talisker is bettered by the extra attention it has received, although the amoroso does transform it into a sweeter and smoother malt.

TALISKER 10 YEAR-OLD 45.8%

The Islands representative for the Six Classics.

Nose	Sea-weedy, spicy, peppery. Undertones of sherry and malt and citrus fruits.
Palate	A rounded flavour with more peat than seaweed coming through. Very chewy and full bodied.
Finish	A warm, peppery finish that goes on and on.
Comment	A big whisky deserving its accolades. Perhaps the most drinkable of the heavily peated malts.

Style   G

TALISKER 1986 DISTILLER'S EDITION 45.8%

Finished in amoroso sherry wood

Nose	TCP, briny and sharp. Wine notes. A touch peppery. Oaky.
Palate	Briny. Heavy peat and heavy body.
Finish	Long peppery finish - slightly dry.
Comment	Not a patch on the standard 10 year-old. Perhaps no adulteration is required with this one?!

Style   G

Region Islands

It will come as no surprise to anyone that has been to Skye or at least seen a map of Scotland to hear that the United Kingdom's weather comes from the west. The battered, scattered and weather-scarred West Coast of Britain is summed up in the Hebridean Islands of which Skye is the largest. Home to the Clan McLeod and once seat of the Lord of the Isles, the history of Skye is as bloody as its coastline is rugged. Dunvegan Castle, the oldest inhabited castle in Scotland was once the seat of the chief of the McLeod clan who was a very shrewd businessman. Not only was he collecting £45 a year rent from the owners of Talisker but he also demanded 10 gallons of the drink each year - probably to be used as a small aperitif before the real drinking began.

Talisker Distillery sits in the lee of the Hawk Hills not too distant from the imposing and dominating Cuillin Mountains. Talisker began life as a supplement to the farmers who would often have to leave their posts unexpectedly if they were needed on the farm. The distillery became so integral to the way of life on Skye that tokens were issued to workers whether they were distillery workers or tweed-knitters, to be spent in the distillery shop.

As with a number of UDV owned distilleries, Talisker uses outdoor worm tubs rather than condensors to cool the spirit vapours, which some believe contribute toward a heavier spirit.

Producer *The Edrington Group* **Founded** *1897*

Tamdhu was built due to its excellent water source below the distillery and operates three pairs of stills. The maltiness of the whisky prevents it being overlooked too much, and in today's climate of masking the distillery's character with cask finishing whenever possible it is nice to find a whisky that has stayed true to its roots.

Tamdhu makes all its lightly peated malt in its Saladin maltings. (see next page) It is another malt whisky that is intended as a 'filler' for blends and this it does with consummate ease. However, some expressions from the independent bottlers have shown a side to Tamdhu that is far more appealing. With a few more years in the wood Tamdhu can lose its boyish good looks and enter adulthood with all guns blazing.

TAMDHU 40%

The whisky is 8 - 10 years old.

Nose	Very malty and spirity. Sweet biscuits and undertones of orange liqueur.
Palate	Chewy malt taste, quite oily.
Finish	A nice, uncomplicated finish.
Comment	Not much happening in this Speyside malt, but pleasant nonetheless.
Style	**C**

Region Speyside

The late 19th Century was a very popular time for the building of distilleries, especially in Speyside where the reputation of the whisky was growing each year. In 1896 no less than three distilleries were to be built in Knockando alone. These were Imperial, Knockando and Tamdhu. Tamdhu was to have no expense spared and after raising £18,200 to fund the distillery the eminent distillery architect and inventor Charles Doig was brought in to design and build it.

The distillery seems to have been unaffected by the Pattison crash of 1898 and such was the reputation of the spirit that Highland Distillers bought it in 1899 just two years after opening. Under Highland Distillers rule the distillery prospered and despite a long closure between 1927 and 1945 the distillery was expanded to four stills in 1972 and then to six stills in 1975.

At this time the distillery was largely rebuilt including a new visitors centre built in the old Dalbeallie Station and Saladin maltings capable of malting 220 tons of barley at a time. This satisfies all of Tamdhu's requirements and also provides for many other distilleries in the area.

The Saladin malting system was a progression of the traditional malting floors. The germinating barely is turned by a continuous automated system within long shallow troughs, rather than by hand.

The barley is then allowed to dry in the traditional way within a kiln heated with locally cut peat, the peat reek being allowed to infuse with the barley. Very few distilleries still have Saladin maltings, most obtaining their barley from industrial maltsters who use large capacity drum maltings.

Producers *Kyndal Spirits* **Founded** *1965*

The River Livet was once famed as the breeding ground of the best whiskies and the concentration of distilleries is testimony to the fame. Tamnavulin (Tam na voolin) is a nice whisky and sings the praises of the quality of the area near the river. The mothballing of Tamnavulin in 1995 will leave a gap in the Kyndal Spirits range when stocks dry up but no doubt this has already been taken into consideration. naturally it is hoped the distillery will re-open at some future date.

The distillery operated six stills and used very lightly peated malt that was brought in from commercial maltings.

From my notes it is easy to see why the whisky is used in blends as it gives all-round pleasurable experiences from the nose to the finish. This is perhaps another whisky that given a little more exposure could find greater favour as a single malt. There are a number of aged Stillman's Drams available on the market, rare but well worth the search.

TAMNAVULIN 12 YEAR-OLD 40%

Nose   Grassy, earthy. Sharp. Honey-maltiness. Nutmeg. Buttery.

Palate   Honey. Malty. Quite light and sweet. Dry and round.

Finish   A mustard finish, long and warming with a creamy floral aftertaste.

Comment   A very enjoyable dram. The palate and finish are perfect hedonistic material.

Style   A

Region Speyside

Meaning 'mill on the hill', Tamnavulin was built in 1965 on the banks of the River Livet (the only distillery to do so). Tamnavulin Distillery was built large by Invergordon Distillers with an annual capacity of around 1.5 million gallons of alcohol. Taking its water from the springs rising in the hills to the west of the distillery appropriately called Westertown, the water is then stored in an underground reservoir and pumped to the distillery via an underground pipe. The water taken from the River Livet is used for cooling purposes only.

An old wool mill was turned into a visitors centre and the waterwheel that powered the machinery was also restored although the distillery has been mothballed since 1995. Invergordon Distillers were bought out by Jim Beam Brands and is now controlled by Kyndal Spirits.

***Producer** Burn Stewart Distillers* **Founded** *1798*

Tobermory typifies a gentle island whisky with just a hint of a sea breeze. It is only very recently that the non-aged version of Tobermory was replaced with the 10 year-old. There are aspects of the younger version that I miss; the apples and pears for instance. But the new 10 year-old will not disappoint those drinkers looking for an island style whisky.

Tobermory is made with completely non-peated barley which is ferried across from Pencaitland having travelled from Leith. However, the Mishnish Loch which supplies the water for the making of Tobermory contains heavily peated water resulting in a hint of peat in the finished product. The four bulbous stills have an unusual S shaped lyne pipe allowing only the lighter spirit to get through!! Maturation takes place in ex-bourbon and ex-sherry casks in warehousing on the mainland at Deanston near the Trossachs .

TOBERMORY *10* YEAR-OLD *40%*

Nose	Malty. Briny with a wave of smoke. Honey and spices.
Palate	Light to medium. Mini explosion of peppery smoke. Chewy.
Finish	Medium finish, warming. Long peppery aftertaste.
Comment	One of the gentler island malts without being overly soft.

Style   E

***Region** Islands*

Tobermory, like Oban, sits on the sea front of a small fishing bay. Unlike Oban the village of Tobermory was built before the distillery. Indeed the planning applications of John Sinclair were rejected a year before it is believed the distillery was built. The distillery was originally called Ledaig (pronounced Lay check) meaning 'safe haven' but with constant changes in ownership and silent periods it was inevitable that the distillery would change its name.

Sinclair kept the distillery in his name until 1837 and after changing hands a number of times fell under the control of the DCL. DCL kept the distillery operating from 1916 - 1930 and then mothballed the distillery removing much of the equipment. The distillery lay silent for forty-two years until it was revived, albeit naively, by Ledaig Distillery (Tobermory) Ltd. The acquisition was during a terrible recession and the consortium lasted only three years before closing Tobermory. Oddly enough the distillery was revived by the Kirkleavington Property Co of Cleckheaton, Yorkshire. Until this time production had been brief and often interrupted. When Burn Stewart acquired the distillery and all of the stock for £800,000 in 1993, production had only been carried out in eight of the previous 63 years!

Over the years the distillery has been used as a maturation house for Mull cheese and when Burn Stewart bought the distillery they were aware that warehousing would have be to carried out in Tobermory's sister distillery Deanston in Doune. This was due to the fact that the warehouses had been sold previously and turned into flats. I don't see what the problem is though, who wouldn't like a cask of whisky maturing in their front room?

Producer *Tomatin Distillery Company* **Founded** *1897*

Tomatin has always been a 'filler' whisky, a malt whisky meant for blending and it is not surprising to learn that a very high percentage of Tomatin whisky makes its way into blends all over the world. What does get bottled as single malt is very promising; a medium bodied whisky that allows a rich malty taste to develop.

With water from the Allt na Frithe (Free Burn), Tomatin is a lightly peated malt which is distilled via two of twenty three large stills. The spirit is matured in ex-bourbon and ex-sherry casks.

Perhaps if Tomatin single malt was given a little more time and development then it is quite possible that the malt could grow in status. Certainly at the moment with Tomatin 10 year-old made available only in small quantities it is unlikely it will get the recognition it deserves.

TOMATIN 10 YEAR-OLD 40%

Nose	Rich malt, cognac notes. Fruit trifle, caramel and sherry.
Palate	Malty, sherried. Medium bodied yet quite delicate.
Finish	Quick finish but warming.
Comment	If Tomatin concentrated a little more on developing its single malt whisky it could be quite a dram. Shows a lot of potential.
Style	**D**

Region *Highlands*

Established in 1897, Tomatin was part of the whisky boom that was halted a year later when Pattison's of Leith was liquidated and the entire Scotch industry found that the market was swamped with whisky. Tomatin continued distilling despite the state of the industry and progress continued up until the Second World War. After this, Tomatin's chequered history led it through strange times of expansion and then liquidation in 1986 when it became the first Scottish distillery to be wholly owned by Japanese investors.

During all of this uncertainty Tomatin quietly became the largest distillery in Scotland housing 28 stills with an output capable of producing in one month (over 400,000 gallons) what some distilleries make in a year. Tomatin though, has always been a blending whisky and has not had much success to date with the 10 year old.

This has meant that the drop in sales over recent years with regard to blends (about 5% each year while malts have increased sales by about 15% each year) has led to more than half of the 28 stills becoming obsolete. Tomatin have had to adjust their use of space and already are dismantling 16 of the 28 stills to make way for a new visitor's centre which will open in 2002.

Tomatin is still one of the largest working distilleries in Scotland. It is a remarkable visit as it was once the most automated distillery in Scotland. It was said that there was more investment in machinery per worker than on an oilrig. Despite all of this automation the distillery is still practicing the time honoured traditions and nothing has really changed in the production of a most underrated malt whisky. Tomatin has never been and probably never will be the prettiest distillery in Scotland. But the welcome you will receive will be second to none.

Producer Angus Dundee **Founded** *1965*

As Tomintoul was built later than most other distilleries that are around today, much care and attention went into the location of the distillery. It has always been understood (probably from day one) that the water source is paramount to the success of a distillery. The builders of Tomintoul monitored the Ballantruan Spring for more than a year, measuring flow and temperature, to ensure a steady supply of clean soft water for the distilling process.

A lightly peated malt is used with distillation being through two pairs of fairly large stills. The whisky is matured on site along side the River Avon in predominantly ex-bourbon casks although some ex-sherry casks are also used.

It is awkward talking about the past tastes of Tomintoul as the distillery is so young and also as the new owners will have a real energy for making the most of their distillery. So we must look to the future for Angus Dundee and Tomintoul. They have a good product and with some care and attention this whisky may reach some giddy heights.

TOMINTOUL *10* YEAR-OLD *40%*

Nose	Honey. Orange zest. Malty. Dry and minty.
Palate	Sweet & earthy. Delicious bitterness. Medium body.
Finish	Long peppery finish. Slightly rubbery and oily.
Comment	An accomplished dram that deserves attention from its new owners.
Style	C

Region Speyside

The sixties saw the first whisky boom of the 20th Century although the output of the grain distillers was far exceeding that of the malt distillers. Patent stills that could produce more spirit in a week than most malt distilleries could produce in a year were pumping out nearly 77 million gallons of grain whisky a year in the early sixties. At the same time only 33 million gallons of malt whisky was being made which left a huge shortage in the industry.

To take advantage of this and in order to ensure future supply, two leading Glasgow whisky brokers built Tomintoul. Building started in 1964 and workers forced to carry two-weeks worth of materials due to the constant poor weather affecting the area. The village of Tomintoul is the highest in the Highlands and snow is expected throughout many months of the year.

The distillery and it's sister distillery Fettercairn were incorporated into the Whyte & Mackay company as a result of a merger between the two companies in the early 1970s. Whyte & Mackay enlarged the distillery shortly therafter and continued to operate it until it was bought by Angus Dundee in 2000.

Although not overly pretty to look at, the distillery was built big and it's many warehouses look imposing in the beautiful countryside. Tomintoul has enjoyed some favour from single malt drinkers since its first bottling in 1975 and this looks set to continue with new owners Angus Dundee, who are already running at full capacity.

A first and foremost thank you to the journalists who have done all the hard work in getting whisky noticed on a grander scale. Messrs Michael Jackson, Jim Murray and Charlie McLean are all guilty of paving the way for other writers to try their hand. For this I am eternally grateful.

There are many people behind the scenes who deserve extra special thanks. Especially Fiona Murdoch from The Whisky Shop, Dufftown, Sukhinder Singh from The Whisky Exchange, London, Tom Dingwell from The Dram Room, Newbury and Alex Kraaijeveld.

The photographers, researchers and I, have all received tremendous co-operation while sourcing information, obtaining samples and proofing the text. We were met with great friendliness and hospitality at every distillery visited, which has made the project all the more enjoyable and rewarding. One distillery deserves a special mention in having me around for a week enabling me to gain a deeper understanding of distillation. Thank you to Stuart and Jackie Thompson, "Yogi", "Dugga", "Wardie" and "Penfold" from Ardbeg. The whole Scottish whisky industry deserves an accolade not just for producing such a fine spirit but also for its commitment to go above and beyond.

Finally thank you to Conrad Townson, Shaun Templeman, Milroy's of Soho and to everyone, friends, family and supporters who will hopefully be buying the book.

A part from the sheer enjoyment of drinking single malt whisky, it is also fun and interesting to sample the many different expressions coming from the different regions, or the same region or even the same distillery. Each malt having it's own unique characteristics.

Interestingly a malt's appeal can vary depending on many things i.e. whether it is sampled at any given time of day, location or setting etc. In addition, your preference may vary, for example you may prefer a Lagavulin on a cold winters evening by a smoky pub fire then perhaps a Glengoyne in a fine restaurant after a delicious meal.

These blank tasting sheets can therefore be used to record your findings of a specific favourite at different times or to record the various whiskies as you try them over the years. Alternatively you might find these pages invaluable if you are attending a whisky tasting event.

You may wish to use all or only some of the information fields but here is a guide set to the type of information you may choose to record. E.g.:

Name of malt	Bowmore
Alcohol	43%
Expression	Mariner 15 year-old
Occasion	After dinner, winter evening, anniversary
Date	Either date of purchase or date of sampling
Where purchased	The Whisky Exchange
Price	£27.50
Nose	Rich peatiness, burnt heather, complex.
Palate	Full bodied, smoky, slight saltiness.
Finish	Fresh, long.
Comments	Excellent after a meal.
Score	This is your chance to record a verdict.

NAME OF MALT Bowmore .... 43 ....%

EXPRESSION *Mariner 15 year-old* OCCASION *After dinner* DATE *10/01*

WHERE PURCHASED *The Whisky Exchange* PRICE *£27.50*

NOSE *Rich peatiness, burnt heather, complex.*

PALATE *Full bodied, smoky, slight saltiness.*

FINISH *Fresh, long.*

COMMENTS *Excellent after a meal.* SCORE *7/10*

USING THE TASTING NOTE PAGES

YOU MAY FIND IT HELPFUL TO CONSULT THE LIST OF KEY TASTING WORDS IN ASSISTING YOU TO DESCRIBE YOUR FINDINGS:

Apple	Fruitcake	Prunes
Aromatic	Ginger	Rich
Balanced	Herbal	Ripe
Bite	Honey	Round
Bitter	Iodine	Salty
Buttery	Leather	Seashore
Caramel	Lemony	Sea weedy
Chewy	Lively	Sherry
Chocolate	Long	Short
Citrusy	Luscious	Shortbread
Cocoa	Malty	Smoke
Coffee	Menthol	Smooth
Complex	Nutmeg	Soft
Creamy	Nutty	Spices
Dried fruit	Oak	Sweet
Dry	Oily	Sour
Elegant	Peat	Toffee
Firm	Peppery	Vanilla
Floral	Pipe smoke	Warming
Fresh	Pot pourri	Woody

NAME OF MALT ....%

EXPRESSION .... OCCASION .... DATE............

WHERE PURCHASED .... PRICE............................

NOSE ....

PALATE ....

FINISH ....

COMMENTS .... SCORE.............................

NAME OF MALT ....%

EXPRESSION .... OCCASION .... DATE............

WHERE PURCHASED .... PRICE............................

NOSE ....

PALATE ....

FINISH ....

COMMENTS .... SCORE.............................

NAME OF MALT ....%

EXPRESSION .... OCCASION .... DATE............

WHERE PURCHASED .... PRICE............................

NOSE ....

PALATE ....

FINISH ....

COMMENTS .... SCORE.............................

NAME OF MALT ....%

EXPRESSION .... *OCCASION* .... *DATE* ....

WHERE PURCHASED .... *PRICE* ....

NOSE ....

PALATE ....

FINISH ....

COMMENTS .... *SCORE* ....

NAME OF MALT ....%

EXPRESSION .... *OCCASION* .... *DATE* ....

WHERE PURCHASED .... *PRICE* ....

NOSE ....

PALATE ....

FINISH ....

COMMENTS .... *SCORE* ....

NAME OF MALT ....%

EXPRESSION .... *OCCASION* .... *DATE* ....

WHERE PURCHASED .... *PRICE* ....

NOSE ....

PALATE ....

FINISH ....

COMMENTS .... *SCORE* ....

NAME OF MALT ....%

EXPRESSION .... OCCASION .... DATE.............

WHERE PURCHASED .... PRICE.........................

NOSE ....

PALATE ....

FINISH ....

COMMENTS .... SCORE...........................

NAME OF MALT ....%

EXPRESSION .... OCCASION .... DATE.............

WHERE PURCHASED .... PRICE.........................

NOSE ....

PALATE ....

FINISH ....

COMMENTS .... SCORE...........................

NAME OF MALT ....%

EXPRESSION .... OCCASION .... DATE.............

WHERE PURCHASED .... PRICE.........................

NOSE ....

PALATE ....

FINISH ....

COMMENTS .... SCORE...........................

NAME OF MALT ....%

EXPRESSION .... *OCCASION* .... *DATE*...............

WHERE PURCHASED .... *PRICE*............................

NOSE ....

PALATE ....

FINISH ....

COMMENTS .... *SCORE*.............................

NAME OF MALT ....%

EXPRESSION .... *OCCASION* .... *DATE*...............

WHERE PURCHASED .... *PRICE*............................

NOSE ....

PALATE ....

FINISH ....

COMMENTS .... *SCORE*.............................

NAME OF MALT ....%

EXPRESSION .... *OCCASION* .... *DATE*...............

WHERE PURCHASED .... *PRICE*............................

NOSE ....

PALATE ....

FINISH ....

COMMENTS .... *SCORE*.............................

To order more blank pages or copies of The Malt Whisky Guide – www.gwpublishing.com or Tel: 01256 814060

NAME OF MALT ....%

EXPRESSION .... OCCASION .... DATE............

WHERE PURCHASED .... PRICE............................

NOSE ....

PALATE ....

FINISH ....

COMMENTS .... SCORE............................

NAME OF MALT ....%

EXPRESSION .... OCCASION .... DATE............

WHERE PURCHASED .... PRICE............................

NOSE ....

PALATE ....

FINISH ....

COMMENTS .... SCORE............................

NAME OF MALT ....%

EXPRESSION .... OCCASION .... DATE............

WHERE PURCHASED .... PRICE............................

NOSE ....

PALATE ....

FINISH ....

COMMENTS .... SCORE............................

NAME OF MALT ....%

EXPRESSION .... OCCASION .... DATE.............

WHERE PURCHASED .... PRICE............................

NOSE ....

PALATE ....

FINISH ....

COMMENTS .... SCORE..............................

NAME OF MALT ....%

EXPRESSION .... OCCASION .... DATE.............

WHERE PURCHASED .... PRICE............................

NOSE ....

PALATE ....

FINISH ....

COMMENTS .... SCORE..............................

NAME OF MALT ....%

EXPRESSION .... OCCASION .... DATE.............

WHERE PURCHASED .... PRICE............................

NOSE ....

PALATE ....

FINISH ....

COMMENTS .... SCORE..............................

NAME OF MALT ....%

EXPRESSION .... OCCASION .... DATE..............

WHERE PURCHASED .... PRICE...........................

NOSE ....

PALATE ....

FINISH ....

COMMENTS .... SCORE..............................

NAME OF MALT ....%

EXPRESSION .... OCCASION .... DATE..............

WHERE PURCHASED .... PRICE...........................

NOSE ....

PALATE ....

FINISH ....

COMMENTS .... SCORE..............................

NAME OF MALT ....%

EXPRESSION .... OCCASION .... DATE..............

WHERE PURCHASED .... PRICE...........................

NOSE ....

PALATE ....

FINISH ....

COMMENTS .... SCORE..............................

NAME OF MALT ....%

EXPRESSION .... OCCASION .... DATE.............

WHERE PURCHASED .... PRICE...............................

NOSE ....

PALATE ....

FINISH ....

COMMENTS .... SCORE...............................

NAME OF MALT ....%

EXPRESSION .... OCCASION .... DATE.............

WHERE PURCHASED .... PRICE...............................

NOSE ....

PALATE ....

FINISH ....

COMMENTS .... SCORE...............................

NAME OF MALT ....%

EXPRESSION .... OCCASION .... DATE.............

WHERE PURCHASED .... PRICE...............................

NOSE ....

PALATE ....

FINISH ....

COMMENTS .... SCORE...............................

NAME OF MALT ....%

EXPRESSION .... *OCCASION* .... *DATE*..............

WHERE PURCHASED .... *PRICE*............................

NOSE ....

PALATE ....

FINISH ....

COMMENTS .... *SCORE*..................................

NAME OF MALT ....%

EXPRESSION .... *OCCASION* .... *DATE*..............

WHERE PURCHASED .... *PRICE*............................

NOSE ....

PALATE ....

FINISH ....

COMMENTS .... *SCORE*..................................

NAME OF MALT ....%

EXPRESSION .... *OCCASION* .... *DATE*..............

WHERE PURCHASED .... *PRICE*............................

NOSE ....

PALATE ....

FINISH ....

COMMENTS .... *SCORE*..................................

To order more blank pages or copies of The Malt Whisky Guide – www.gwpublishing.com or Tel: 01256 814060

NAME OF MALT ....%

EXPRESSION .... OCCASION .... DATE.............

WHERE PURCHASED .... PRICE.............................

NOSE ....

PALATE ....

FINISH ....

COMMENTS .... SCORE.............................

NAME OF MALT ....%

EXPRESSION .... OCCASION .... DATE.............

WHERE PURCHASED .... PRICE.............................

NOSE ....

PALATE ....

FINISH ....

COMMENTS .... SCORE.............................

NAME OF MALT ....%

EXPRESSION .... OCCASION .... DATE.............

WHERE PURCHASED .... PRICE.............................

NOSE ....

PALATE ....

FINISH ....

COMMENTS .... SCORE.............................

NAME OF MALT ....%

EXPRESSION .... OCCASION .... DATE..............

WHERE PURCHASED .... PRICE...........................

NOSE ....

PALATE ....

FINISH ....

COMMENTS .... SCORE..........................

NAME OF MALT ....%

EXPRESSION .... OCCASION .... DATE..............

WHERE PURCHASED .... PRICE...........................

NOSE ....

PALATE ....

FINISH ....

COMMENTS .... SCORE..........................

NAME OF MALT ....%

EXPRESSION .... OCCASION .... DATE..............

WHERE PURCHASED .... PRICE...........................

NOSE ....

PALATE ....

FINISH ....

COMMENTS .... SCORE..........................

NAME OF MALT ....%

EXPRESSION .... OCCASION .... DATE.............

WHERE PURCHASED .... PRICE...........................

NOSE ....

PALATE ....

FINISH ....

COMMENTS .... SCORE...........................

NAME OF MALT ....%

EXPRESSION .... OCCASION .... DATE.............

WHERE PURCHASED .... PRICE...........................

NOSE ....

PALATE ....

FINISH ....

COMMENTS .... SCORE...........................

NAME OF MALT ....%

EXPRESSION .... OCCASION .... DATE.............

WHERE PURCHASED .... PRICE...........................

NOSE ....

PALATE ....

FINISH ....

COMMENTS .... SCORE...........................

To order more blank pages or copies of The Malt Whisky Guide – www.gwpublishing.com or Tel: 01256 814060

NAME OF MALT ....%

EXPRESSION .... OCCASION .... DATE.............

WHERE PURCHASED .... PRICE..............................

NOSE ....

PALATE ....

FINISH ....

COMMENTS .... SCORE...............................

NAME OF MALT ....%

EXPRESSION .... OCCASION .... DATE.............

WHERE PURCHASED .... PRICE..............................

NOSE ....

PALATE ....

FINISH ....

COMMENTS .... SCORE...............................

NAME OF MALT ....%

EXPRESSION .... OCCASION .... DATE.............

WHERE PURCHASED .... PRICE..............................

NOSE ....

PALATE ....

FINISH ....

COMMENTS .... SCORE...............................

NAME OF MALT ....%

EXPRESSION .... OCCASION .... DATE..............

WHERE PURCHASED .... PRICE................................

NOSE ....

PALATE ....

FINISH ....

COMMENTS .... SCORE...........................

NAME OF MALT ....%

EXPRESSION .... OCCASION .... DATE..............

WHERE PURCHASED .... PRICE................................

NOSE ....

PALATE ....

FINISH ....

COMMENTS .... SCORE...........................

NAME OF MALT ....%

EXPRESSION .... OCCASION .... DATE..............

WHERE PURCHASED .... PRICE................................

NOSE ....

PALATE ....

FINISH ....

COMMENTS .... SCORE...........................

To order more blank pages or copies of The Malt Whisky Guide – www.gwpublishing.com or Tel: 01256 814060